SYRIA STABILIZATION STABILIZES

DR. JAMIL EFFARAH

authorHOUSE®

AuthorHouse™
1663 Liberty Drive
Bloomington, IN 47403
www.authorhouse.com
Phone: 1 (800) 839-8640

Published by AuthorHouse 11/25/2019

ISBN: 978-1-7283-3762-3 (sc)
ISBN: 978-1-7283-3761-6 (e)

CONTENTS

INTRODUCTION

Syria destabilization stabilizes after eight years of a running destructive war to overthrow President Bashar Al-Assad failed and President Al-Assad stayed in control to lead the stabilization and reconstruction of Syria. It is important to learn more about Syria and how plans to destruct and destabilize Syria started and why.

The secret CIA report entitled *"Bringing Real Muscle to Bear Against Syria"* that took place on **September 14, 1983** was approved for release on May 5, 2008, that is, after 25 years, it says:

"Syria is at present has a hammer lock on US interests both in Lebanon and the Gulf – through closure of Iraq's pipeline thereby threatening Iraqi internationalization of the war. The US should consider sharply escalating the pressures against Assad through covertly orchestrating simultaneous military threats against Syria from three Border States hostile to Syria: Iraq, Israel and Turkey. Iraq, perceived to be increasingly desperate in the Gulf War, would undertake limited military (air) operations against Syria with the sole goal of opening the pipeline. Although opening war on a second front against Syria poses considerable risk to Iraq. Syria would also face a two-front war since it is already heavily engaged in the Bekaa, on Golan and in maintaining control over a hostile and restive population inside Syria."

"Israel would simultaneously raise tensions along Syria's Lebanon front without actually going to war. Turkey, angered by Syrian support to Armenian terrorism, to Iraqi Kurds on Turkey's Kurdish border areas and to Turkish terrorists operating out of modern Syria, has often considered launching unilateral military operations against terrorist camps 1 northern Syria. Virtually all Arab States would have sympathy for Iraq."

"Faced with three belligerent fronts, Assad would probably be forced to abandon his policy of closure of the pipeline. Such a concession would relieve the economic pressure on Iraq, and perhaps force Iran to reconsider bringing the war to an end. It would be a sharp blow to Syria's prestige and could affect the equation of forces in Lebanon."

The paper was signed by Graham E. Fuller [1], It also says that "Syria continues to maintain a hammerlock on two US interests in the Middle East:

Syrian refusal to withdraw its troops from Lebanon ensures Israeli occupation in the south;

Syria closure of the Iraqi pipeline has been a key factor in bringing Iraq to its financial knees, impelling it towards dangerous internationalization of the war in the Gulf.

Diplomatic initiatives to date have had little effect on Assad who has so far correctly calculated the play of forces in the areas and concluded that they are only weakly arrayed against him. If the US is to rein in Syria's spoiling role, it can only do so through exertion of real muscle which will pose a vital threat to Assad's position and power."

The CIA released report covers the situations in Iraq, Israel, Turkey and the USSR with an addendum which ended by the following paragraph: "One can argue that Iraq – after concluding

---

[1] **Graham E Fuller is a former vice chairman of the National Intelligence Council at the CIA, a former senior political scientist at RAND, and a current adjunct professor of history at Simon Fraser University. He is the author of numerous books about the Middle East, including *The Future of Political Islam. A World Without Islam, and Turkey and the Arab Spring, Leader in the Middle East* (April 2014). He has lived and worked in the Muslim world for nearly two decades. He is also author of a memoir, *Three Truths and a Lie*, and a novel, Breaking Faith (February 2015) about the U.S. imbroglio in Pakistan.**

a war with Iran – will revert to its old hard line radical ways. This is open to debate. Although Iraq will then be less vulnerable, it will still need to remain on guard against Iranian influence and power throughout the Gulf. It will still wish to challenge its rival Syria.

With signs of a shift in policy from the US, Iraq could be encouraged to join in a regional threat against its enemy Syria. Although Israeli involvement is not appealing to Iraq, Iraq knows that Syria has few Arab sympathies these days. Even the mere perception by Syria that the US was improving relations with Iraq, talking of some assistance, and that regional military forces –Israel, Turkey, Iraq – were gearing up against Syria it could have major impact upon Syrian ambitions. At this stage Syria has no one – except possibly Israel – to challenge it effectively in the region.

It is also very interesting to read the article which Professor Fuller [2] where he argues that *"only continuing American commitment to its deepest international ideals is what makes the US what it is; that if we fail to uphold our ideals we are left with no organizing national principle—and thus no national purpose."* (Never mind that these "ideals" are upheld on a highly selective, transient, cherry-picked basis.)

But do we really believe that the US will atrophy as a society in the absence of *"maintaining global values?"* It would be sad to think that US greatness depends on constant intervention and war in the name of the global order.

How long can the US go on "generously," supplying international order? Perhaps we are indeed doomed to watch an increasingly Darwinian world out there, operating without Big Brother. But the handwriting is on the wall: few in the world still support American policing of the world—or perhaps policing by any single state.

If policing is required (and there may be an occasional role for it) it will ever more likely involve a consortium of major international players—at a bare minimum EU, China, and Russia. The UN Security Council, when it can agree, also plays an important role. Indeed, these three powers are determined to deny the US any further monopoly of international power. And that was true before Trump.

In the end, how do we think about history? A process is of gradual advancement? Or anarchy kept at bay only by great powers? Does history have any "meaning," any trajectory? Or, as an earlier British statesman debunked the whole notion: "history is just one damn thing after another."

Back to Syria, to find out that recently the conflict between Qatar and Saudi Arabia surfaced, we start to learn more about the United States support for creating an Islamic State in Iraq and Syria, ISIS or Al-Dawlat Al-Islamia Fi al-Iraq wa Ash-Sham (DAESH) to destroy Hezbollah, topple Al-Assad, install a puppet regime and extend the comfort to Occupiers of Palestine.

It does not seem logical to have the United States directly support the terrorist Islamic State in Iraq and Syria. The idea of United States and its allies supporting ISIS is shocking to most people and creates a lot of painful disagreements. You see, to overthrow President Bashar Al-Assad in Syria, the US elites could not openly arm Al-Qaeda and ISIS. That's where *Saudi Arabia and Qatar* come into play. These two countries would buy the weapons from the U.S. and ship them to the terrorists in Syria mostly via Turkey and some through Jordan (Turkey borders Syria on the north; Jordan on the south).

The Wikileaks founder, Julian Assange noted that the US government had never acknowledged governments of Middle East nations had financially supported ISIS, instead arguing such support was isolated to *"some rogue princes using their cut of the oil money to do whatever they like, although the government disapproves"*. In the email sent on August 17, 2014, Julian Assange pointed to that

---

[2] **Graham E. Fuller, ""*Global Disorder - What Are the Options?*" August 22, 2017**

email exchange between presidential hopeful Hillary Clinton wrote to her campaign manager, John Podesta, who at that time worked under President Barack Obama, to help put "pressure" on Qatar and Saudi Arabia regarding the countries' alleged support for the terrorist group ISIS, by stating that "*Qatar and Saudi Arabia are providing clandestine financial and logistic support to ISIS and other radical Sunni groups in the region,*" Hillary Clinton wrote: "*We need to use our diplomatic and more traditional intelligence assets to bring pressure on the governments of Qatar and Saudi Arabia, which are providing clandestine financial and logistic support to ISIL and other radical Sunni groups in the region.*"

Again, the US vice president, John Biden, told his audience [3] – point blank – that "*America's Sunni allies are responsible for funding and arming Al Qaeda-type extremists in Syria.*"

In the Q&A session following Biden's speech, he answered a question to whether the United States should have acted earlier in Syria identifying "moderate rebels"; a portion of the answer was: "*The fact of the matter is the ability to identify a moderate middle in Syria was – there was no moderate middle because the moderate middle is made up of shopkeepers, not soldiers – they are made up of people who in fact have ordinary elements of the middle class of that country. ... that our biggest problem is our allies – our allies in the region were our largest problem in Syria. The Turks were great friends – and I have the greatest relationship with Erdogan, which I just spent a lot of time with – the Saudis, the Emiratis, etc. What were they doing? They were so determined to take down Assad and essentially have a proxy Sunni-Shia war, what did they do? They poured hundreds of millions of dollars and tens, thousands of tons of weapons into anyone who would fight against Assad except that the people who were being supplied were Al-Nusra and Al-Qaeda and the extremist elements of Jihadis coming from other parts of the world. Now you think I'm exaggerating – take a look. Where did all of this go? So now what's happening? All of a sudden everybody's awakened because this outfit called ISIL which was Al-Qaeda in Iraq, which when they were essentially thrown out of Iraq, found open space in territory in eastern Syria, work with Al-Nusra who we declared a terrorist group early on and we could not convince our colleagues to stop supplying them. ...Now we have – the President's been able to put together a coalition of our Sunni neighbors, because America can't once again go into a Muslim nation and be seen as the aggressor – it has to be led by Sunnis to go and attack a Sunni organization*".

Furthermore, Wesley Clark[4] *says: "the United States created ISIS to destroy Hezbollah"*... and "*our friends and allies funded ISIS.*" He added: "*ISIS got started through funding from our friends and allies. People will tell you in the region that if you want somebody who will fight to the death against Hezbollah, you don't put out a recruiting poster saying 'sign up for us we're going to make a better world.' You go after zealots and you go after these religious fundamentalists. That's who fights Hezbollah. It's like a Frankenstein.*"

Even more bizarrely, both the *U.S. and Israel* have admitted that they view ISIS positively since it was/is helping them in the regime change plot against Assad. Not to mention that Israel's relationship with ISIS is beyond suspicious.

I do not forget John Kerry, the US Secretary of State, who admitted that "*the U.S. sought to use ISIS as leverage against Assad during negotiations,*" and in the same audio, Kerry talks about how the U.S. has spent a lot of money and efforts overthrowing Assad; and how Putin came in and weakened ISIS.

Yet again, Presidential candidate Evan McMullin tweeted on August 15, 2016 that his role in CIA was "*to go out and convince Al-Qaeda operatives to instead work with us.*"

---

[3] **speaking at the John F. Kennedy Jr. Forum at Harvard University's Institute of Politics, on Thursday (September 27, 2014)**
[4] *Wesley Clark* **Former US four star** *General* **and Supreme Allied** *Commander* **of NATO interviewed on CNN, February 21, 2015**

All the top people in the U.S. government knew and acknowledged the roles of Saudi Arabia and Qatar in funding ISIS. This statement is not speculative; it is the truth and based on facts that I intend to prove in writing this book.

I am convinced that the above-mentioned evidences can be put together to convince the Americans and the World Community that the United States of American support ISIS by putting together flight to tens of thousands of Al-Qaeda Jihadists (fighters) from all over the world to topple President Bashar Assad who said "no" to a Qatar pipeline through Syria.

I intend in this book to speak about Syria before and after the conspiracy to destabilize it, its destabilization and its stabilization that includes clarification for the rise and fall of the Islamic State in Iraq and Ash-Sham (ISIS) or Levant (ISIL) and what was and is still going on in Syria and the rest of region.

I will start by giving a bird's eye view of Syria followed by a short historic review to the origin of the ideology of ISIS and Al-Qaeda or the extreme Islamic Jihadist-Salafist (Wahhabi) movement that grew through the years up to the recent time when they are used as tools of destabilization by the CIA and the American Administration to achieve the American superiority worldwide starting with the elimination and destabilization of the Middle Eastern countries to control the sources of oil and gas production on one hand and to serve the Israeli ambition to create "Greater Israel" from the Euphrates River in Iraq to the Nile River in Egypt on the other. After all, ISIS does represent the Israeli Security Intelligence Service that played a major role that failed in the plan to destabilize Syria.

Since 1967, Israel has illegally occupied part of Syria, the Golan Heights. In 1981, the Israeli regime annexed Syria's land even though the entire world, including the United States, refuses to recognize the Golan Heights as anything other than part of Syria, except when President Trump reversed half-century-old U.S. policy, when he bestowed it illegally as a gift to the Zionist state Israel and on June 17, 2019, Israel announces new Golan Heights settlement named "Trump Heights"

Since 1978, Egypt has normalized relations with Israel to the point of becoming a partner against Palestine. Jordan whose Hashemite monarchy craved prestige in the Arab world but lost a great deal of it for opposing revolutionary Arab nationalist parties, made a similar peace partnership agreement with the Israeli occupiers in 1994.

With Israel occupying Lebanon into the new millennium, this left Syria as Israel's only powerful rival in the Arab world. This was especially the case after the Gulf War weakened Iraq.

Israel has always enthusiastically backed so-called regime change in Syria and continued its efforts to either co-opt or subdue parts of the Arab world, a process which has successfully rendered their token statements about Palestine as geo-politically useless.

In 2011, the US broke its tacit accommodation with Syria and provided arms and financing to its local Islamist clients for an uprising which seized control of most of the countryside and major cities, including half of Damascus' neighborhood. Fortunately, Assad sought the support of Russia, Iran and the Lebanese Hezbollah fighters. Over the next eight years, the US-EU backed terrorists were defeated and forced to retreat, despite massive military, financial and logistic support from the US, EU, Israel, Saudi Arabia and Turkey.

Syria has survived and reconquered most of the country, it was able to secure an armed-alliance with strategic allies who succeeded in neutralizing domestic insurgents. Due to the steadfastness of the Syrian Arab Army, Syria's secular constitution which has enabled a united front against jihad and imperialism and due to military assistance from Russia and Iran, Syria has not fallen and nor will it. In 2015 the whole situation changed with Russian intervention at the Syrian government's request. Russians got involved as they saw the potential economic damage that a pipeline through

Syria from the Gulf would cause, as well as, their wish to improve their regional influence, including their naval base in Syria.

Syria remains committed to liberating the occupied Golan Heights as well as remaining the only steadfast supporter of Palestine in the Arab world. This much was confirmed during Syria's recent address to the UN General Assembly in September 2017.

"Civil war" does not apply to Syria which was not divided if it fought a civil war. In reality, if sect killing another sect, Syria should be divided according to sectarian lines. But Syria managed to stay one country, united country, united society, because a civil war will not go on for seven or eight years continuously without dividing the country.

The Syrian government succeeded to survive in controlling the majority of Syria with all the Syrian diversities or with different spectrums of the Syrian society. What took place in Syria from the very beginning are mercenaries, Syrians, and foreigners being paid by the West and its allies in the region in order to topple the government. This is the reality, the mere reality, the very stark reality. Everything else is just masks to cover the real intentions.

Today, the Syrian government restored over 85 per cent of Syrian territories and its main goal is to liberate Syria and regain its unity, as well as the return of its displaced citizens by improving their rights and conditions. Nowadays, Syria is the only Arab state that defies western expansionism in the Middle East and Syria was and still is a pillar of support for Arab resistance in Iraq, Lebanon and Palestine.

I expect that this book is essential for anyone seeking a deeper understanding for the cause of the current social turmoil and political violence ravaging the Arab-Islamic world, mainly the Syrian Arab Republic.

CHAPTER ONE
SYRIAN ARAB REPUBLIC

T hroughout its history, Syria's political and economic importance has been largely attributable to its position at the crossroads of three continents and several cultures. Since ancient times, Syria has been the center of trade between the east and the west. This trade and the location of the country have for millennia made Syria a melting pot of diverse beliefs, cultures, ideas and talents.

Since 2011, destruction descended on the Syrian Arab Republic from all over the world, but as terrorism is curtailing, the real Syria will return to take its leading role in the region.

Syria's area includes about 184,180 square kilometers (71,500 sq. mi) of deserts, fertile plains, and mountains with a borderline of 2,413 km (1,500 mi). It is a country located in the Middle East on the shore of Mediterranean Sea and bordered, from the north down to the west, by Turkey, Iraq, Jordan, Palestine, and Lebanon.

Specific demographic data for Syria is unreliable. Some minority groups are defined primarily by religion, others by ethnicity, and some are relatively recent immigrants. Many of them can also be found in neighboring countries. Physical and human geography have been major determining factors in Syria's social fabric: city, desert, mountain and sea. Until the present century, social divides between town dwellers, peasants and Bedouin, and the conflict between the latter two, were almost as important as religious differences.

Syria's population was estimated by "World Bank" in 2011 at 20.8 million and was growing at an estimated rate of 2.4 percent in 2004. The annual growth rate from 1990–2002 was 2.6 percent. About 52 percent of the population was urban as of 2002, with a growth rate of 3.1 percent.

Syria is one of the most densely populated countries in the Middle East (57 people per square kilometer in 1986 and about 363 per square kilometer in 2004), but there are significant regional variations. The population is concentrated along the coast In the west, In the south around Damascus, the capital, and in the Euphrates River Valley in the northeast. 499,189 Palestinian refugees reside in Syria by the end of 2012 according to the United Nations Relief and Works Agency for Palestine Refugees (*UNRWA*), and 1.2 million Iraqi refugees since the U.S.-led invasion of Iraq in 2003. In addition, Syria before the crisis had already some 170,000 internally displaced people, mostly from the Golan Heights.

Most Syrian institutions were kept intact, mainly its educational system that deserves mentioning here:

The Education System in Syria

Despite the recent crisis, Syria still has a solid basic education system. All Syrian schools providing primary and secondary education, including private and the UNRWA schools are closely supervised by the Syrian Ministry of Education. This UN organization used to provide primary, secondary and post-secondary professional education for 44,000 Palestinian students in Syrian refugee camps.

The Syrian education ministry is directly responsible for the curriculum and the learning materials used. The language of education is Arabic. All public primary and secondary education are free. Education is mandatory between the ages of 6 and 15 (up to the 9th grade).

Up until 2002 there was a three-part system in primary and secondary education (6+3+3 years). With each phase a diploma is included. The first phase was 6 years of primary school, (the second phase 3 years of general secondary education (lower level) and the third phase 3 years of general secondary education (upper level).

Since 2002 the first two phases have been merged and this phase is mandatory for all pupils aged 6 to 15. This phase of education concludes with a centrally sets national examination. Upon passing this exam, pupils are awarded the Basic Education Certificate (شهادة الدراسة التعليم الأساسي).

Depending on the results achieved in the national exam for the Basic Education Certificate, pupils can either pursue Vocational Secondary Education or General Secondary Education. The Syrian state provides 95% of secondary education, with the rest provided by private institutions and the UNRWA. Vocational Secondary Education is provided by technical schools and is further divided into a number of main specializations such as industry, trade and agriculture. These programs of study conclude with a Technical/Vocational Secondary Education Certificate. Diplomas have different names depending on the subject area, such as the Industrial Secondary School Diploma, the Secondary School of Commerce Diploma, and the Secondary School of Agriculture Diploma.

The upper level of general secondary education lasts 3 years and pupils are usually aged 15 to 18. This phase of education concludes with a centrally set exam conferring the which (الشهادة الثانوية) General Secondary Education Certificate is also referred to as the Baccalaureate. This phase of education prepares pupils for academic higher education, and in principle those who complete it successfully are admitted to universities and other higher education institutions. The first year is a common introductory year, after which students choose a subject cluster in either arts or sciences. The academic year runs from September to June and has 32 teaching weeks, excluding exam weeks

Post-secondary education

Following completion of vocational secondary education students can either start work or apply to a Technical or other Intermediate Institute. These educational institutions offer programs with a professional focus in industry, agriculture, technology, administration, economics, business, teacher training for primary and lower level secondary education, transport, tourism etc.

These study programs have a nominal duration of 2 years. In Syria these programs are considered higher vocational education. There are 16 ministries involved in providing this education, though most Intermediate Institutes come under the Ministry of Education and the Ministry of Higher Education. Policymaking is the responsibility of the Supreme Council of Intermediate Institutes, which is part of the Ministry of Higher Education.

Study programs conclude with a Technical Diploma Certificate or Certificate of Associate Degree, often also translated as the Certificate of Licensed Assistant

Admission criteria vary considerably. Intermediate Institutes connected to a university usually require a General Secondary Education Certificate or a Technical Secondary Education Certificate with an exceptionally high score. At the other end of the spectrum, there are Intermediate Institutes which accept students with a low score on their Technical Secondary Education Certificate or even those who don't have one.

Admission to higher education

The General Secondary Education Certificate (also known as the Baccalaureate) is a prerequisite for admission to higher education in Syria. In principle, any student who passes their final exam can continue on to higher education. Individual faculties do set minimum final scores each year, and applicants need to have taken the right subject cluster for their study program. Students who have taken the science subject cluster can usually apply for admission to any study program offered within higher education.

Those who take the arts subject cluster can only apply for degree programs in literature, art, humanities, economics and law. Students with very high scores for the Technical Secondary Education Certificate can be admitted to university bachelor's degree programs in a comparable area, but this is rare.

Admission to the faculties of medicine, dentistry, architecture and natural sciences requires high scores on the final exam for the General Secondary Education Certificate. The scores required for admission vary each year and are set centrally by the University Admissions Committee at the Council of Higher Education (Ministry of Higher Education). No entrance examinations are required for admission into higher education, but certain programs might have a draw procedure. Some faculties set additional requirements, such as having a passing grade in a second foreign language or a particular course. Students with very high scores on their final exams can be admitted to university bachelor's degree programs in a comparable subject area.

Admission criteria vary considerably. Intermediate Institutes connected to a university usually require a General Secondary Education Certificate or a Technical Secondary Education Certificate with an exceptionally high score. At the other end of the spectrum, there are Intermediate Institutes which accept students with a low score on their Technical Secondary Education Certificate or even those who don't have one.

Syrian higher education is provided by universities and higher institutes. Higher education institutions are the responsibility of the Ministry of Higher Education. For example, any developments related to a curriculum must be approved by the Ministry. New private universities also have to adhere to certain guidelines when they're set up and are closely monitored in their initial phases. The Council for Higher Education is the overarching body coordinating the education provided by higher education institutions. Syria has both public and private universities. There are currently 7 public universities and 20 private universities. Education at public universities in Syria is free and is provided in Arabic.

The University of Damascus was founded in 1903 and is the oldest and largest university. The Syrian Virtual University is an unusual public university. It was founded in 2002 by the Ministry of Higher Education to offer online education in partnership with international institutions. The programs offered by the Syrian Virtual University are usually vocational. Private universities have been around since 2001. These must be recognized by the Ministry of Higher Education before they can deliver any education. Tuition fees are charged and the education may be provided in English as well as in Arabic. Higher institutes are regarded as 'centers of excellence' and are usually directly supervised by public universities or the Ministry of Higher Education. Admission requires higher scores on the General Secondary Education Certificate than for public universities. Higher institutes offer degree programs at the Bachelor's, Master's and PhD level. The number of students attending these institutes is relatively low.

The Syrian Healthcare System

The Syrian government of the Baath Party has placed an emphasis on healthcare as reported that Syria was the first state to have established a 21st-century healthcare system, but funding levels have not been able to keep up with demand or maintain quality. Syrian healthcare was established to meet the health needs of the Syrian populations who were protected by a fully developed health system and civil infrastructure. Health expenditures in Syria reportedly accounted for 2.5 percent of the gross domestic product (GDP) in 2001.

Syria's health system was relatively decentralized and focuses on offering primary healthcare at three levels: village, district, and provincial. According to the world Health Organization (WHO), in 1990 Syria had 41 general hospital (33 public, 8 private), 152 specialized hospitals (16 public, 136 private), 391 rural health centers, 151 urban health centers, 79 rural health units, and 49 specialized health centers; hospital beds totaled 13,164 (77 percent public, 23 percent private), or 11 beds per 10,000 inhabitants. The number of state hospital beds reportedly fell between 1995 and 2001, while the population had an 18 percent increase, but the opening of new hospitals in 2002 caused the number of hospital beds to double. WHO reported that in 1989 Syria had a total of 10,114 physicians, 3,362 dentists, and 14,816 nurses and midwives; in 1995 the rate of health professionals per 10,000 inhabitants was 10.9 physicians, 5.6 dentists, and 21.2 nurses and midwives?

Despite overall improvements, Syria's health system exhibits significant regional disparities in the availability of healthcare, especially between urban and rural areas. The number of private hospitals and doctors increased by 41 percent between 1995 and 2001 as a result of growing demand and growing wealth in a small sector of society. Almost all private health facilities are located in large urban areas such as Damascus, Aleppo, Tartous, and Latakia.

Before the war Syria's hospitals were the envy of the Middle East. The average life expectancy was 75, higher than in many parts of the world. Nine out of every 10 medicines provided by the country's extensive network of public and private clinics were made by the country's own flourishing pharmaceutical industry. Back then, Syrians could expect a long healthy life, and care and comfort in times of sickness.

Today and after eight years of war, the healthcare system in Syria has totally, totally broken down. Syria is now in an unprecedented situation. It is the first state ever to have established a fully functioning, highly effective, 21st-century healthcare system – and then seen it collapse.

Two-thirds of the country's hospitals have been affected by the fighting and 40 per cent of them have been destroyed or rendered altogether useless. Ninety per cent of the pharmaceutical industry, which used to pump out drugs not only for domestic use but for export to 50 countries globally, is defunct. The government is now dependent on medical supplies from its allies – Russia, Iran and, to a lesser extent, Cuba and Honduras, as well as UN-coordinated aid coming in through Damascus and one border crossing with Iraq.

In areas completely out of government control, smaller aid agencies and non-government organizations (NGOs) are the main source of drugs and equipment, ferried in from neighboring countries.

Near the front lines, medical facilities have been targeted, along with medical professionals, by forces on both sides, under the grim logic that the fewer doctors there are to put to put people back together, the fewer men will come back to fight.

Syria's population, like the rest of the developed world, had for years been lifted up by the safety net of modern medicine. But currently that it has been taken away, people are falling hard. Around six million are refugees in their own country, living in crowded, unhygienic temporary shelters, bombed out buildings, or wherever they can – served only by undersupplied, undermanned field clinics.

The Syrian Economic System

Syria's economic structure and politics are highly centralized. Since the rise of the Ba'ath party in 1963, centralization of the economy has been followed in accordance to the socialist ideologies of the party and its leaders.

The main source of foreign income for the Syrian economy is from the export of oil, estimated at 155,000 bbl./day in 2010. Other exports include crude oil, minerals, petroleum products, fruits and vegetables, cotton fiber, textiles, clothing, meat and live animals, wheat – estimated to total $10.13 billion.

Between 1990 and 1995 major oil discoveries and economic reforms were taken by the Syrian government.

In 2003 the Syrian economy suffered when the allies invaded Iraq leading to significant drop in the number of tourists and a stop in the flow of cheap Iraqi oil and commissions received from Saddam's regime which was also a main source of income for Syria during the UN embargo, thanks to the Oil for Food program and through smuggling. The economy shrank 2.14% in that year.

Syria's economy then recovered in 2004 following high oil prices in the international market and a rebound from the Iraq crisis, growing 6.719%. It grew consistently 4% - 5% until 2010, managing a decent showing during the Great Financial Crisis.

Syria's GDP (on a Purchasing Power Parity basis) was US $105.324 billion in 2010. This makes Syria No. 65 in world rankings according to GDP (PPP), US Dollars in year 2010. In 2011, GDP is forecasted to reach US$112.56 Billion. Forecasters believe that Syria will see improved growth over the next few years, in the 5% to 6% range annually.

Syria's economy faces the challenges of lack of investment due to its government and lack of required reforms to enable investments. Syria also suffers a high unemployment rate that is put at 9.2 percent in 2010 by the IMF. Other groups believe this is understated, however, with some estimating that it is as high as 20%.

Depleting oil reserves is also a problem for Syria, as well as water supplies affected by pollution and public and external debt which makes up 98 percent of its GDP. Syria also has $21.55 billion in external debt which is equivalent to 45 percent of its income. Such debts and their servicing charges place a constraint on the Syrian economy. They also reduce Syria's ability to acquire new loans from international credit agencies.[5]

It is important to mention that Syria supplies almost all of its own food needs. The proportion of the population working in agriculture has decreased significantly from 50 percent in 1970, to 30 percent in the 1980s, to 23 percent today. Despite this decline, production has increased, thanks in large part to the dam at Tabqa, which has allowed for increased irrigation. Half of the workforce is employed in industry and mining. There is less of a gap between the rich and the poor in Syria than there is in many other countries, and as more of the population gains access to education, the middle class continues to expand.

---

[5] **Information taken from an article written by Liz Zulliani, March 20, 2011 in the "Economic Watch: follow the money", www.economywatch.com/world_economy/syria/structure-of-economy.html)**

The Syrian Political System

Syria held its first parliamentary elections in 1932. All the candidates were hand-picked by the French, but once elected; they declined the constitution France had proposed for the country. Anti-French sentiment grew when France turned over control of the Syrian province of Alexandretta to Turkey. It was exacerbated by the promise of independence in 1941, which was not delivered until five years later.

After independence, civilian rule was short-lived, and the early 1950s saw a succession of coups, after which Syria formed the United Arab Republic with Egypt in 1958. This represented an effort to keep the Arab states more powerful than Israel, but it disintegrated in 1961, when Syria came to resent the concentration of power in Egypt.

After experimenting in a union with Egypt's Jamal Abdel Nasser, creating "the United Arab Republic" between 1958 and 1961 when separation took place. The Arab Socialist Ba'ath Party came to power in Damascus and worked on building a revolutionary program of emancipation from colonial lethargy as well as a foreign policy which defended Arab interests against interlopers, colonists and outside threats allowing Syria to embrace modern Arabism during the 8th of March, 1963 when the March Revolution was declared.

The situation was worsened by the Six Day War against Israel in 1967 and the Black September disagreement with Jordan in 1970.

Hafez al-Assad, the leader of a radical wing of the Arab Socialist party, the Ba'ath, seized control in 1971. In 1992, he won his fourth consecutive bid for election with 99.9 percent of the vote. During the Gulf War in the early 1990s, the country aligned itself with the anti-Iraq coalition, thus winning the approval of the United States and removing itself from the United States' government's list of nations supporting international terrorism. Hafez al-Assad died in June 2000. The younger of his two sons, Bashar, just months before assuming his father's position, he married to the British born Asma, who worked as an investment banker before meeting her in Britain in 2000. Asma's father is Fawaz Akhras from Homs, Syria; he worked as the First Secretary at the Syrian Embassy in London.

Secular Syria has its Syrians tend to identify primarily with their religious group or sect; however, as the majority of the country is Sunni Muslim, this creates a strong feeling of cultural unity. Modern-day Syria is in part the result of geographic lines drawn by the French in 1920, and there is still a strong pan-Arab sympathy that defines national identity beyond the current borders. In 1967, after the six-day war, "Israel" took the Golan Heights, a Syrian territory. The Syrian national identity is based in part on the concept of defending and reclaiming this land.

Syria is ethnically fairly homogeneous (80 percent of the population is Arab). Religious differences are tolerated, and minorities tend to retain distinct ethnic, cultural, and religious identities. The Alawite Muslims (about a half-million people) live in the area of Latakia. The Druze is a smaller group that resides in the mountainous region of Jebel Druze. The Ismailis are an even smaller sect that originated in Asia. The Armenians from Turkey are Christians. The Kurds are Muslim but have a distinct culture and language, for which they have been persecuted throughout the Middle East. The Circassians, who are Muslim, are of Russian origin and generally have fair hair and skin. The nomadic Bedouins lead a lifestyle that keeps them largely separated from the rest of society, herding sheep and moving through the desert, although some have settled in towns and villages.

Ancient Syria

Ancient Syria is one of the oldest inhabited regions in the world with archaeological finds dating the first human habitation at 700,000 B.C. years ago.

In its early written history, the region was known as Eber Nahri (across the river) by the Mesopotamians and included modern-day Iraq, Syria, Jordan, Lebanon, and Palestine (collectively known as The Levant).

It is most likely that the modern name "Syria" derives from "Assyria" (which comes from the Akkadian "Ashur" and designated the Assyrian's chief deity).

Most archeologists found out that the two most important cities in ancient Syria were Mari and Ebla, in the region of Sumer [6] (Mari in the 5th and Ebla in the 3rd millennium BC) and both of which used Sumerian script, worshipped Sumerian deities, and dressed in Sumerian fashion. Both of these urban centers were repositories of vast cuneiform tablet collections, written in Akkadian and Sumerian, which recorded the history, daily life, and business transactions of the people and included personal letters. When Ebla was excavated recently in 1974 the palace was found to have been burned and, as with Ashurbanipal's famous library at Nineveh, the fire baked the clay tablets and preserved them. At Mari, following its destruction by Hammurabi of Babylon in 1759 BC, the tablets were buried under the rubble and remained intact until their discovery lately in 1937 when Max Mallowan[7] excavated Tell Brak[8]. Together, the tablets of Mari and Ebla provided archaeologists with a relatively complete understanding of life in Mesopotamia in the 3rd millennium BC.

Syria during Christ Era

The notion of a single omnipotent and omnipresent God is borrowed from Assyrian predecessors. The Judeo-Christian-Islamic tradition that began in the Holy Land was not a total break with the past; but grew out of religious ideas that had already taken hold of Late Bronze and Early Iron Age northern Mesopotamia, the world view of the Assyrian kingdom, which would spread its faith as well as its power right across western Asia over the course of the following centuries.

This heritage was held by the people of Syria who, it is claimed, could have influenced depictions of kings, battles, and events as recorded in the Old Testament and even the vision of the risen God Jesus as given in the New Testament. Saul of Tarsus, who would later become the apostle Paul and then Saint Paul, was a Roman citizen of Tarsus in Syria who had seen a vision of Jesus while on route to Damascus, Syria. The first major center of Christendom rose in Syria, at Antioch, and the first evangelical missions were launched from that city and became known as Christianity.

---

[6] **The region of Sumer was the southernmost region of ancient Mesopotamia (modern-day Iraq and Kuwait) which is generally considered the cradle of civilization? The name comes from Akkadian, the language of the north of Mesopotamia, and means "land of the civilized kings."**

[7] **Sir Max Edgar Lucien Mallowan, (1904-1978), was a prominent British archaeologist, specializing in ancient Middle Eastern history.**

[8] **Tell Brak (Nawar) was an ancient city in Syria. Its remains constitute a hill (tell or mound) located in the Upper Khabur region, near the modern village of Tell Brak, 50 kilometers north-east of Al-Hasaka city. The city's original name is unknown. During the second half of the third millennium BC, the city was known as Nawar**

No doubt the Bible is derived from Mesopotamian sources and owes its existence to the people of Syria, who would have helped to spread Mesopotamian culture.

Modern Syria

Based on my own experience, I would like to introduce President Bashar Al-Assad as representative of modern Syria in an article I have written in 2001 about "***Dr. Bashar Assad: A New Generation of Leadership in Syria***"[9]. This article says: How much Americans know about Syria since Dr. Bashar Al-Assad assumed the Syrian presidency? Many claimed that he would be a man of economic and social reform, yet few believed that political reforms in their true sense would occur in a country so long ruled by autocratic military rule.

Since the Ba'ath Party's rise to power in March 1963, no one dared voice opinions, question the government, or show the slightest sign of dissatisfaction or dissident. It was difficult for a society accustomed to political debate and conduct to keep their mouths shut and their opinions to themselves. The Ba'ath Party enforced a system of martial law on the country that has not been lifted since, justified by the fact that Syria is in a constant state of war with the Zionists, occupiers of Palestine, and needs emergency laws to be on constant alert. Martial law has enabled the state to arrest citizens with no warrant and dismantle all non-governmental organizations.

But with Bashar Al-Assad in power, he has managed to surprise everyone, both his closest adversaries and loudest critics. For the first time in four decades, citizens have begun to discuss politics in public, and feel secure enough to give their points of view on matters, even if these contradict those of the regime. Political reforms first began showing in September 2000, when 99 Syrian intellectuals signed a manifesto in Damascus calling on the regime to end martial law, grant political freedoms, and release all political prisoners. Syrian intellectuals made it clear that they want democracy. They want to open the door for the freedom of expression, the freedom for clear thinking and constructive writings. With the use of Internet, the world/globe gets closer and smaller, and the time for intellectuals has come to unshackle their hands and untie their tongues.

Since April 1999, Nawal Yazigi, a Communist Party activist, has been holding intellectual forums at her Damascus residence where journalists, analysts, and thinkers meet and lament the deteriorating conditions in Syria. They asked for dismantling of the Ba'ath Party and for changing the Constitution to break the one-party rule in Syria. The issue, often raised by anti-Ba'ath intellectuals, used to remain a topic for private discourse, one that no one dares bring out in the open, but now more comments are coming out into public discourse.

The young president, Bashar Al-Assad made it clear that he accepts the fact that the Ba'ath Party may be appealing to some but it is not a religion to be followed by all, so he allowed other parties to come into existence, open offices and practice their creeds. Member of Parliament started to address the assembly and condemn "the political and economic monopolies" in place for the past 40 years. They started talking against military dictatorship, asked for marginal political conduct, and began a campaign for restoring civil society to Syria.

Based on creating new horizons, we believe that the foundations for a globally competitive in industrial sectors are fairly sound. The building blocks for these foundations include investor-friendly policies and strong communications channels in the public sector. Bashar Assad's new

---

[9] **Dr. Jamil Effarah, "*Think Palestine: To Unlock U.S. Israelis & Arabs Conflicts*" (vol. one) AuthorHouse, Bloomington, Indiana, 2007, page 100**

leadership shows the determination to integrate Syria into the world economy. We start to observe, on the micro level, the process of adopting new technologies and seeking improvements to gain greater efficiency and higher quality is well established. As for the public sector, implementing policies designed to support both local manufacturers and potential investors and to include minimum trade efficiency (specifically bureaucratic procedures) industrial zones, and export promotion initiatives.

Bashar Assad declared his intention of establishing a "more ideal" Syrian-Lebanese relation, and as a result, had 54 Lebanese political prisoners transferred from Syrian jails to Lebanese ones to stand trial in their own country. Unlike his father, who used to respond with wide-scale waves of arrests of Lebanese citizens on Lebanese soil, many Lebanese officials welcomed Bashar's move. A move that portrayed Bashar Assad as not a violent man; and that he is sincerely working for change from within his own country. The move might undermine Syria's power in Lebanon, and eventually lead to decreasing Syrian influence in Lebanon.

Bashar Al-Assad is trying to break the hold of the old-fashioned decision-makers, after 40 years of oppression, and promote to positions of authority a generation of young and able men and women, who are free of the complexities of the past and are working for change. Various pieces of reform adopted in Syria during 2000. This trend is still going on at full speed, mainly, to allow private banks. Under the new banking law that went into effect on January 20, 2001, new banks can be set up as private joint stock companies or as partnerships between the government and the private sector. Syrians would own at least 51 percent of the new firms, with Arab investors in general and Lebanese banks in particular are expected to have the best chances to be the first non-Syrians to enter the sector. Syria has five state-run banks that would continue operating, but competition will doubtless lead to their being refurbished.

On a regional level, Syria signed a free-trade pact with Iraq expecting to increase trade between them to $1 billion this year from $500 million in 2000, all within the limited exchanges permitted by UN sanctions. Syria and Iraq also plan to build a new oil pipeline, as the old one between them, unused since 1982, is no longer economical. Planned capacity of the new pipeline is around 1.4 million barrels per day; it would be built in two stages: the first from the Iraqi border inside Syrian territory and the second in Iraq.

As well as the deal to build a $1 billion gas pipelines linking Syria, Egypt, and Iraq, the three countries forming a market of about 120 million people. These are indicative of a further opening up to regional trading partners. The signing of a 115 million Euros credit was the second European Investment Bank loan to Syria in two months to finance Syrian electricity projects (the first, in December, was worth 75 million Euros). This is in contrast with the US "national interests", which has still not fully mended fences with Syria after the troubled 1980s and, unfortunately, it seems that the US may not do so before "the Syrians settle their differences with Israel".

Still Bashar has to face a back-breaking problem the unemployment among Syria's college graduates is at 30 percent, and the country must provide 270,000 jobs per year for its population of 17 million, expected to double by 2020.

I would like to introduce a real event took place in February 1958. The late Syrian President Shukri al-Kuwatly, while signing the union charter with Egypt, addressed Jamal Abdel Nasser by saying. *"Mr. President, you have taken over a people where every single one of them thinks he is a politician. 50 percent claim to be natural leaders, and 25 percent believe they are prophets. And at least 10 percent, Mr. President, act as if they are gods."* An exaggerated rhetoric, but very reflective to the nature of the Syrian Arab people in action that Bashar has to deal with to convince the US and The

Zionist occupiers of Arab lands that the price of peace is very cheap if the Zionists withdraw from the Syrian-occupied territories to its 1967 borders.

I believe that my article in 2001 had a passive reflection before the American and Zionist-Israeli interests and ambitions to occupy and destroy Syria after what they have done in Iraq that the past events showed how the Al-Qaeda and ISIS destructive ideology are used to serve the Zionists and the American ambitions.

President Bashar Al-Assad Inauguration Speech

President Bashar Hafez Al-Assad's inauguration speech [10] came as a landmark strategy and mechanism of action at all levels and fields. Bashar reiterated Syria's ever cling to the realization of just and comprehensive peace on the related United Nations Security Council resolutions, the full return of the land to line of June 4 1967 lines, calling on Mideast peace sponsor to actively and evenhandedly be engaged in the process and for more Arab solidarity, cooperation and coordination.

In his speech, President Al-Assad expressed special thanks to all Syrians, men and women, old and young, inside and outside Syria who bestowed upon him their trust through voting in the referendum and through their active participation in this national duty. He thanked his people for all the love and loyalty they expressed that granted him strength and optimism for the future.

The President intended to do his very best to lead Syria towards a future that fulfils the hopes and legitimate ambitions of the Syrian people.

From the beginning, President Bashar made it clear that he is not after any post nor to avoid any responsibility. To him, the post is not an end but a means to achieve an end. But since the Syrians have honored him with their choice of being the president of the Republic. He occupied the position that he determined to maintain and cherish to be strong by it and through it. This position that never changes is the position from which he will serve his people and his country.

President Bashar said that in order to be constructive in his criticism he has to be objective in his thinking as objectivity dictates that he shall view each topic from more than one perspective and under more than one circumstance. Hence, he will analyze it in more than one way and then he may reach more than one possibility, or at least the best possibility or the closest to the truth.

He has to stop ushering criticism with the objective of beseeching people or of inviting people to clap hands for him or with the aim of provocation or malice. This is a waste of energy and time that he can well do without. When he says constructive criticism and an objective opinion this will necessarily mean to view the topics under criticism in a complete and comprehensive fashion in a way that enables him to see the positive points as well as the negative ones. In this way he will be able to increase the positive points at the expense of the negative ones and this is the only way to development.

Al-Assad said that there is a need for coordination and complimentary orientation among measures and steps taken in all fields; and that transparency is an important thing and he supports such an endeavor but through a proper understanding of the content of the idiom and of the ground on which it might be based. To the President, prior to being an economic or a political or an administrative case, transparency is a state of culture, values and social habits. This poses a question and a requirement in the meantime that he should ask himself before he addresses it to others.

---

[10] **July 7, 2000**

Al-Assad's aspirations will not be properly fulfilled unless he emphasizes the role of institutions in the Syrians lives. To him. the institution is neither a building nor a system that governs nor the persons who work in it; rather, it is first and foremost, the institutional thinking that considers every institution, however small it might be and whatever its domain may be, a representative of the entire country, its reputation and its civilized outlook. Institutional thinking acknowledges that institutional work is a joint and not a personal work, a work that is based on honesty, sincerity and on using time to the maximum extent, on putting public interest above personal interest, and on putting the mentality of a state above the mentality of the tribe. It is the logic of cooperation and openness to others, and it is inseparable from the democratic thinking which has many things in common with it in various places. This means that democratic thinking enforces and strengthens institutional thinking and work.

President Bashar added that he has to respect law because it guarantees the state's respect for the citizen and the citizen's respect for the state. The rule of law guarantees the freedom for the Syrians and the freedom of others. He has to fight waste and corruption taking into account that each kind of work will necessarily entail a percentage of unintentional mistakes which should not worry him but he should try not to allow their recurrence. He insisted to distance himself from chaos and wasting time and to commit himself truly and sincerely to his work and to double his efforts in order to make up for what has been lost.

The President intends to give up the idea of uprooting the status quo in totality instead of working to develop and improve it basing his work on the view that human life has no ultimate truth. No matter how bad the reality might be it must carry within it some good things, and no matter how good or excellent it might appear it will not be pure from misgivings.

Despite this deteriorating state of relations among Arab countries which might prompt some to be pessimistic and others to be frustrated President Bashar will not surrender to the feeling of utter hopelessness to achieve any breakthrough in this regard. He insists that neither he surrenders to this current reality nor he will be satisfied with it.

Concerning the United Nations, he believes that the policy of adhering to the principles of international legitimacy requires the United Nations to carry out its mission as mentioned in its Charter in an objective way and away from different points of influence that might limit the implementation of these principles in the best way possible in order to reach a world with no conflicts and no points of tension, a world where peace, justice and democracy prevail among countries and in which dialogue is deepened and broadened among different civilizations in the world of today.

President Al-Assad ends his speech by saying: *"The man who has become a president is the same man who was a doctor and an officer and first and foremost is the citizen."*

CHAPTER TWO
UNDERSTANDING THE EXTREME ISLAMIC SALAFIST IDEOLOGY

Al-Qaeda is but one manifestation of this decades-old Extreme Islamic-Salafist or (Takfiri) ideology and movement. The global Islamic-jihadist movement was and remains more than just al Qaeda—or ISIS. It consists of individuals worldwide, some of whom have organized, who seek to destroy current modern Muslim societies and resurrect in their place a "true Islamic society"- that is an Islamic "Umma" ruled by a Caliphate - through the use of armed force. America and the West have no chance of success in this conflict unless they understand that this movement is their true and proper adversary.

Al-Qaeda, the Islamic State, and the global Salafist-jihadist movement together are stronger today than they have ever been. The Qaeda (Salafist-jihadist) groups are becoming active in Iraq, Syria, Yemen, Somalia, Libya, and Mali as well as in Afghanistan, Egypt, Tunisia, and Nigeria. Furthermore, both ISIS and al Qaeda started to pursue deadly attack capabilities to target their creators in the West.

Al-Qaeda believes that participation in armed conflict to create a true Islamic polity is obligatory for all true Muslims. The theological foundations of Al-Qaeda have existed since at least the 13th century. The Islamist movement that began at the end of the 19th and carried into the 20th centuries resurfaced these arguments, which Muslims largely rejected as extremist or, in some cases, heretical.

Today's Al-Qaeda or ISIS movement is not a new phenomenon nor has its ideology fundamentally changed in recent years. Adaptations in the messaging of that ideology, its placement into colloquial language and distribution through new mediums, are only new means of distribution and not reasons for the expansion of the extreme Islamist Salafist-jihadist movement. Al Qaeda put the ideology on the internet with the late cleric Anwar al Awlaki [11], and ISIS monopolized social media, but the global movement is also strong in areas without internet penetration. The message itself and the groups propagating it have hardly changed in the past decade, yet its fortunes have risen dramatically since 2011. We must look elsewhere to understand why the movement is growing in strength today.

The modern Al-Qaeda movement formed during the Afghan jihad. Muslim and Arab countries provided thousands of volunteer fighters known as "Afghan Arabs", who wished to wage Jihad against the atheist communists. Notable among them was a young Saudi named Osama bin Laden, whose Arab group eventually evolved into al-Qaeda. This fight, and the ones that followed, provided experiential learning that refined the movement's strategic thought. Al-Qaeda, the extreme Islamic groups have come together repeatedly after Afghanistan in Algeria, Bosnia, Tajikistan, Somalia, Egypt, Chechnya, again in Afghanistan, and then in Iraq, Syria and Lebanon—but each time remained isolated.

Al-Qaeda leaders know that the movement's strength derives from its relationship with the Muslim community. The movement seeks to conduct a global insurgency, a task that requires

---

[11] Anwar al Awlaki is a radical American Muslim cleric of Yemeni descent was linked to a series of attacks and plots across the world - from 11 September 2001 to the shootings at Fort Hood in November 2009. Awlaki's overt endorsement of violence as a religious duty in his sermons and on the internet is believed to have inspired new recruits to Islamist militancy. After surviving several attempts on his life, he was killed in a US drone strike in western Yemen on 30 September 2011.

popular support—or at least toleration—to end its isolation in the Muslim world. Its leaders have focused on the relationship with that community for decades, but prior efforts to engage were either futile or short-lived.

Local Sunni communities rejected Al-Qaeda extreme ideology repeatedly. The ultra-conservative interpretation of Islam ran afoul of local custom, of local Islam. The call to violent jihad lacked resonance. Coercive tactics backfired, and the introduction of new, alternative systems of governance proved reversible. The failed Al-Qaeda leaders generally died. Those who have survived have learned lessons from all these encounters. However, the real reason for the current success of the extreme Islamist movement is the transformation of conditions in the Muslim-majority world since 2011. Events outside the movement's control removed a primary obstacle to its ability to build local support, by mobilizing Sunni communities in local, national, and regional conflicts that caused and resulted from the "Arab Spring".

Dissatisfaction with governance across the Middle East and North Africa gave rise to popular uprisings that destabilized neighboring regions. Domestic conflict in many Arab states shifted rapidly from a question of political rights to one of individual or communal survival. The movement, whose leaders had studied prior setbacks for how to improve, was primed to offer help to communities that suddenly felt facing existential threats. It gained acceptance at a basic level simply by providing limited amounts of governance and security in places where governments and security forces had either collapsed or become enemies of the people they ruled.

Al-Qaeda movement got advantages from what was called "Arab Spring" to revive in Iraq and Syria after the United States'war in Iraq that energized al-Qaeda, its affiliated groups, and like-minded jihadists around the world. *"The United States invaded an oil-rich Muslim nation in the heart of the Middle East, the very type of imperial adventure than bin Laden has long predicted is the "Crusaders' "long-term goal in the region. The American invasion deposed the secular, socialist Saddam, whom bin Laden had long despised, ignited Sunni and Shia fundamentalist fever in Iraq, and provoked a classic "defensive" Jihad that has galvanized Jihad-minded Muslims around the world.* [12] " The jihad against the Soviets in Afghanistan was a critical turning point because it transformed the ideology into a global movement. The Afghan-Soviet war was the first conflict in the modern era that drew in Muslim recruits of all nationalities.

The Mujahedeen's (Muslim fighters) success in Afghanistan proved that victory was possible and also that it was possible to cause an Islamic emirate to be established in order to lay the foundation for the future Caliphate.

The Iraqi war resulted in having funds powering upon Jihadists from Gulf countries, mainly from Qatar and Saudi Arabia, as reported that the CIA and the US Administrations encouragement. Al-Qaeda, under the name of ISIS, brilliantly seized an unexpected opportunity and is now positioned where it has never been before in its decades of existence, but not for too long.

The elements of American power now operate against merely a fraction of the movement. They may destroy that fraction but will not destroy or even defeat the movement itself.

After supporting ISIS, the United States administrations did not know how to develop a new strategy to counter the extreme Islamist movement as a whole—not just al-Qaeda, ISIS, the off-shoot of al-Qaeda, or even local groups that seemingly present the greatest threats. The US foreign policy did not understand this movement from its ideology to its military strengths to its popular outreach and governance. It did not proceed from an understanding of why the movement has

---

[12] **Peter L. Bergen "The Osama bin Laden I know" Free Press, a division of Simon & Schuster, Inc. New York, 2006, page 350**

gained strength recently after foundering for so many years. It must start by redefining the enemy at the most basic level. The American strategic focus on the components of the movement—from al Qaeda to ISIS to the ideology—has been misplaced.

The Origin of the Salafist-Jihadist/Al-Qaeda Members

The Salafist-Jihadist are orthodox Sunni Muslims who believe the Muslim community, the Umma, has strayed from true Islam which they define as the Islam practiced in the time of the companions of the Prophet and his early followers. They hold that Muslims must return to the fundamentals of Islam contained entirely within the Qur'an and the Hadith (sayings and actions of the Prophet) in order for the Umma to be as strong as it was in the *Islamic Golden Age* that was the era in the history of Islam, traditionally dated from the 8th century to the 15th century, during which much of the historically Islamic world was ruled by various caliphates, and science, economic development and cultural works flourished. It seems today that those extreme Muslim Salafist-Jihadists are committed to the use of armed force to achieve their aims. So, Al-Qaeda movement believes that the only way to revive true Islam is to guide their actions in rigid allegory to the initial struggle to spread Islam during the age of the Prophet and the Rightly Guided Caliphs.

Al-Qaeda or ISIS' ideology carries forward concepts of who can rightly claim to be a Muslim that were first developed when Muslim powers fought one another to the current day. By reading the history books of Islam, scholars can trace elements of Al-Qaeda back to the writings of the 13th century scholar Ahmad ibn Taymiyyah.[13] Ibn Taymiyyah issued a fatwa, religious ruling, that broke from Islamic tradition and authorized the use of force in battle against a group claiming to be Muslim. Twentieth-century Islamists advanced arguments that became a foundational core of Al-Qaeda ideology. These include Mohammed Rashid Rida[14], who called for the restoration of the Caliphate; Abul A'la Maududi[15], who described much of Muslim society's history as un-Islamic or in the state of jahiliyyah (ignorance of Allah's guidance) and called for adherence to shari'a; Hassan

---

[13] **Ibn Taymiyyah, one of the most influential medieval writers in contemporary Islam, where his particular interpretations of the Qur'an and the Sunnah and his rejection of some aspects of classical Islamic tradition are believed by some scholars to have had considerable influence on contemporary Wahhabism, Salafism, and Jihadism; and particular aspects of his teachings had a profound influence on Muhammad ibn Abd al-Wahhab, the founder of the Hanbali reform movement practiced in Saudi Arabia known as Wahhabism, and on other Wahhabi scholars. Ibn Taymiyyah's controversial fatwa allowing Jihad against other Muslims, as it is referenced to by Al-Qaeda.**

[14] **Islamic thinker Muhammad Rashid Rida (1865-1935) was influential in the revival movement of the nineteenth and early twentieth century that influenced and continued to influence Muslim youth. Rida was born in a village near Tripoli in Lebanon.**

[15] **Maududi was the first 20th-century scholar to base his theory on the original founding of Islam. He argued against modernization and Western concepts and reasserted the Islamic concept of the sovereignty of Allah, asserting that nothing was outside of Allah's law. He argued that Islam's purpose was to establish Allah's sovereignty on earth through man— the Caliph—acting by virtue of Allah's delegation of sovereignty to him and bound by shari'a.**

al-Banna[16], the founder of the Muslim Brotherhood; and Sayyed Qutb[17], who wove together tenets from ibn Taymiyyah, Rashid Rida, Mawdudi, and Hassan al-Banna in his book "Milestones" to lay out a plan to return Islam to its roots. Qutb called for a vanguard to lead Muslims in the effort to revive Islam.

This destructive ideology, with its strong dictatorial resonances, holds in the words of its founder, the Indo-Pakistani ideologue Abul A'la Mawdudi that *no single individual, family, a class, a party or any individual living in the state has the right to Hakimiyya [governance], as Allah is the true ruler and holder of real power.*

What is more interesting is that ISIS in Syria gave priority to its conflicts with the Nusra Front and other opposition militias rather than against Assad's forces. Both groups share the totalitarian impulse of the Salafi extreme Islamic movements gave priority to the "government of God" over the will of the people. The question this raises, of course, is: Who will exercise power on behalf of God? Before he was executed by the Egyptian government in 1966, Mawdudi's disciple, the Egyptian Sayyed Qutb, added a revolutionary element to Mawdudi's vision by calling for a jihadist vanguard whose mission was to bring about the "rule of God," if necessary, by force.

Both Qutb and Maudidi sought first to build the umma, by which they meant a new community of righteous Muslims, and then to engage with society writ large to reconvert it to Islam. Qutb's argument for undertaking violent jihad focused on transforming the societies in which his new umma was forming. He claimed that the new umma's experiences would follow the Prophet Mohammed's, predicting that the Muslim states and societies would reject the new community and act against it.

Creation of Current Al-Qaeda

With Soviet forces withdrawing from Afghanistan, the idea of a global jihad suddenly seems possible to Osama bin Laden and some of his top associate to build the base for their aim of Al-Qaeda. Bin Laden moves his base of operations from Pakistan to the Sudan, where he forges links with militants across the Middle East and North Africa who play a role in numerous terrorist attacks, including the 1993 bombing of the World Trade Center.

In February 1998, Bin Laden was expelled from the Sudan; he returned to Afghanistan and

---

[16] **Hassan al-Banna is the Egyptian Islamic leader who founded the Muslim Brotherhood, initially as a youth club stressing moral and social reform. He was born in 1906 in the village of Mahmoudiyya in the northwest Cairo, Egypt. In February of 1949, at 43 years of age, Al-Banna was assassinated**
[17] **Sayyed Qutb (1906-1966) was an Egyptian writer, educator, and religious leader. His writings about Islam and especially his call for a revolution to establish an Islamic state and society greatly influenced the Islamic resurgence movements of the 20th century. Qutb claimed that the umma had been nonexistent for centuries because Muslims had ceased practicing correctly and worshiped false deities in the form of their secular rulers. He dedicated a chapter of Milestones to the creation of the umma, which starts with the creed, the shahada or declaration of faith ("There is no god but Allah, and Mohammed is the messenger of Allah."). Qutb's understanding of the shahada was revolutionary, for he argued that to declare the faith was also to reject any form of human government. He believed that the umma must begin with the creed and separate itself from society, although winning over this society remains keyed. He writes in his introduction to Milestones: "Islam cannot fulfill its role except by taking concrete form in a society."**

issued a fatwa against the United States. Later that year, it was reported that he ordered the U.S. Embassy bombings in Kenya and Tanzania, which kili 224 people.

The Taliban in Afghanistan failed to surrender bin Laden who was accused of masterminding the 9/11 attacks, the U.S. and British forces attacked Afghanistan on October 7, 2001. Most of al-Qaeda members went into Pakistan, where they reorganized and reconstituted and proceeded to play a role in bombings from Bali in 2002 to Madrid in 2004 to London in 2005.

Ayman al Zawahiri [18], an Egyptian leader who had connected himself to Osama bin Laden in the mid-1980s to gain resources for his group in Egypt, pushed for al-Qaeda to support groups seeking to topple the regimes. Zawahiri had bin Laden's ear after Abdullah Azzam's [19] 1989 assassination, and he took al-Qaeda in that direction initially. Azzam's thinking— the defense of Muslim lands—did not disappear, however, and came to be central to al Qaeda's message, especially after 9/11.

Al Qaeda's establishment as a formal organization dedicated to jihad to make Islam victorious across the world was transformational for the Extreme Muslim fanatic movement. It linked global objectives with those of local organizations with national objectives (overthrowing the ruler and state). Yet how to prioritize the fight remained in contention. Azzam's writings indicate that he viewed the next priority for the movement to be other Muslim lands that were under attack by an aggressor.

Abdullah Azzam's ideas continue to reverberate within Al-Qaeda discourse, and his writings remain a source of inspiration for individuals worldwide. Azzam's approach to building a global network by connecting various individuals and groups continued after his assassination in 1989.

Azzam established branches of his "Service Bureau," the organization dedicated to recruiting and training foreigners to fight in Afghanistan, in places such as the United States. This effort created a significant global footprint and produced a group of hardened activists whose beliefs transcended national divisions. Osama bin Laden was but one of many future leaders in this group. Bin Laden rose to prominence within Al-Qaeda movement because he inherited Azzam's transnational networks, not just because he had the money to fund al Qaeda's operations.

On September 2012, Zawahiri called on his followers to exploit the violence in Syria, where rebels are battling President Bashar al-Assad's regime. Seven months later, al Qaeda in Iraq changed its name to the Islamic State of Iraq and ash-Sham (ISIS) to emphasize its growing involvement in the Syrian conflict. But ISIS soon begins to feud with another al Qaeda affiliate in Syria, Jabhat al-Nusra.

The competition between Abu Baker al-Baghdadi [20], leader of ISIS, and Abu Mohammed

---

[18] **Ayman al-Zawahiri, born June 19, 1951, an eye surgeon who helped found the Egyptian militant group Islamic Jihad, was named as the new leader of al-Qaeda on 16 June 2011, a few weeks after Osama bin Laden's death.**

[19] **Abdullah Azzam (1941-1989) was a Palestinian Islamist preacher who helped found al-Qaeda. He is often referred to as the father of global jihad and was instrumental in recruiting foreign fighters to Afghanistan in the 1980s. Azzam theorized that Muslims should fight a single, global jihad against their enemies as opposed to smaller, separate national fights. He served as Osama bin Laden's mentor. It was reported that his theories have also allegedly inspired large scale terrorist attacks and attempts, including the 2009 suicide bombing of a CIA base in Afghanistan, and the 2010 Times Square bombing attempt.**

[20] **Abu Bakr al-Baghdadi is the leader of the Sunni Salafi jihadist militant jihadist organization known as the Islamic State of Iraq and the Levant. Born in Samarra, Iraq on July 28, 1971. On October 3o, 2019, the head of U.S. Central Command, Gen. Frank McKenzie says the body of ISIS leader Abu Bakr al-Baghdadi was buried at sea after last weekend's commando raid in Syria in which al-Baghdadi detonated a suicide vest, killing himself and two young children in order to avoid capture.**

al-Joulani [21], leader of the Nusra Front, seems likely to strengthen the leader of jihadist movement. Unlike the Nusra Front, ISIS excommunicates Islamists who take part in electoral politics, thereby justifying their execution.

On January 3, 2014, As Iraq slides toward civil war ISIS captures the city of Fallujah. *"The police and the Army have abandoned the city,"* a local journalist told the *Washington Post*. *"Al-Qaeda has taken down all the Iraqi flags and burned them, and it has raised its own flag on all the buildings."*

The Caliphate

The Islamic State's emir, Abu Bakr al-Baghdadi, first announced the creation of the caliphate in June, 2014, from the pulpit of Mosul's Grand Mosque. It was based on a utopian vision, dating back to Islam's founding, that was modernized by the Muslim Brotherhood a century ago, hijacked and militarized by radical ideologues, and globalized by Al Qaeda. The Islamic State rejuvenated the jihad after the United States forced Al Qaeda in Iraq underground, in 2007, and killed Osama bin Laden, in 2011. It blitzed across Syria and Iraq, and then recruited tens of thousands of Muslims, from five continents, to govern and protect the new caliphate.

By June, 2014, al-Qaeda, ISIS and its affiliates were able to seize vast swathes of territory in Iraq and Syria and proclaim a 'caliphate'. By these gains in Syria and Iraq, ISIS controlled more territory in the Arab world than at any time in its history.

Such expansion did not leave long and by the first of September 2017, Al-Qaeda was kicked out from Iraq and lost most of the Syrian territories that it controlled.

The quest for a "caliphate" may go on and Muslim fanatics like Al Qaeda members might lay claim to it for a moment, and the believers in a Caliphate for the Islamic State or "umma islamieh" may do the same; but there's always been this Islamic dream of recapturing a certain place and bringing back the caliphate. But I believe that the Caliphate of Islam in modern days went down the drain into extinction.

---

[21] **Ahmed Hussein al-Shar'a, known by Abu Mohammad al-Julani, is the military leader of the Syrian militant group Tahrir al-Sham; he was also the emir of its predecessor organization, al-Nusra Front, the Syrian branch of al-Qaeda. Born in Shheeli, Syria in 1974**

CHAPTER THREE
THE WAR IN SYRIA

The Syrian war has become a proxy war and the deadliest conflict the 21st century has witnessed so far. It is an ongoing multi-sided armed conflict in Syria fought primarily between the government of President Bashar al-Assad, along with its allies, and various terrorist forces opposing the government.

As the Syrian conflict enters its seventh year, more than 465,000 Syrians have been killed in the fighting, more than a million injured and over 12 million Syrians - half the country's prewar population - have been displaced from their homes.

In 2011, what became known as the Arab Spring revolts toppled Tunisian President Zine El Abidine Ben Ali and Egyptian President Hosni Mubarak; that March, peaceful protests erupted in Syria after creating an incident to create chaos. The Syrian government, led by President Bashar al-Assad, responded to the protests violently and in July 2011, some defectors from the military announced the formation of the "Free Syrian Army", a rebel group aiming to overthrow the government, and Syria began to slide into war.

What caused the uprising in Syria?

Many Islamist movements, mainly the Muslim Brotherhood group, were strongly opposing to the Assad's family rule especially when Bashar's father, Hafez al-Assad, in 1982, ordered a military crackdown on them in Hama, which killed many of the Muslim Brotherhood members and flattening much of the city.

Although the initial protests in 2011 were mostly non-sectarian, armed conflict led to the emergence of starker sectarian divisions. Most Syrians are Sunni Muslims, but Syria's security establishment has long been dominated by members of the Alawite sect to which President Assad belongs. The sectarian split is reflected among regional actors' stances as well. Even global warming has been claimed to have played a role in sparking the 2011 uprising.

A severe drought plagued Syria from 2007-10, spurring as many as 1.5 million people to migrate from the countryside into cities, which exacerbated poverty and social unrest giving a well-prepared opportunity to international involvement led by the CIA and the United State Administration.

The International Interference in Syria

On the "Rebels/terrorists" Side

Foreign backing and open intervention have played a large role in Syria's war. An international coalition led by the United States has bombed targets of the Islamic State of Iraq and the Levant (ISIL also known as ISIS) group since 2014.

The US has repeatedly stated its opposition to the Assad government, but has hesitated to involve itself deeply in the conflict, even after the Assad government accused of using chemical weapons in 2013, which former US President Barak Obama had referred to as a "red line" that would prompt intervention.

In October 2015, the US scrapped its controversial program to train Syrian rebels, after it was revealed that it had spent $500m but only trained 60 fighters and only five were left to serve in the program.

In February 2017, the CIA froze funding and logistical support for rebel factions in northern Syria but according to Free Syrian Army (FSA) sources, the funding was restored to a certain extent by late March.

On April 7, 2017, the US carried its first direct military action against Assad's force by launching 59 Tomahawk cruise missiles at a Syrian air force base from which US officials believe "a chemical attack" in Khan Sheikhoun had been launched. Only 39 missiles hit close by with limited losses. It was a fabrication accusation to justify US military intervention, according to President Bashar Assad.

Several Arab states also have provided weapons to rebel groups in Syria; while Sunni-majority states including Turkey, Qatar, Saudi Arabia and others staunchly support the so-called "rebels".

Turkish troops and special forces backed by the "Free Syria Army", launched in August 2016 operation "Euphrates Shield" against ISIL to liberate the strategic Syrian city of Jarablus on the border with Turkey and to stop the advance of Kurdish militia fighters. Turkey's government fears its large native Kurdish population may grow more restive and demand greater autonomy as a result of increased Kurdish control in northeast Syria backed by the US.

In March 2017, Turkey officially ended the Euphrates Shield military operation, but stuck again in April against Kurdish PKK targets in the Karachok Mountains. Turkey's top officials have also criticized the US' decision to arm Kurdish fighters battling ISIL in Syria.

"Israel" also carried out air strikes inside Syria, the latest of which on Damascus and Quneitra.

On the Syrian Government Side

Russia launched in, September 2015, a bombing campaign against what it referred to as "terrorist groups" in Syria, which included ISIL as well as rebel groups backed by western states. Russia has also deployed military advisers to shore up President Assad government's defenses.

At the UN Security Council, Russia has vetoed eight Western-backed resolutions on Syria, while China vetoed six resolutions.

On May 4, 2017 Russia, Iran and Turkey called for the setup of four De-escalation zones in Syria [22], in which Syrian and Russian fighter jets are not expected to fly over for six months. However, as of July 6, the three countries failed to agree on the details of the ceasefire agreement, such as the policing of the four safe zones and their boundaries.

Note concerning Hezbollah in Syria

The involvement in the Syrian War has been substantial since the beginning of armed insurgency phase of the Syrian War and turned into active support to the Syrian Government forces across Syria and troop deployment from 2012 onwards. Hezbollah deployed several thousand fighters in Syria and by 2015 lost up to 1500 fighters in combat. Hezbollah has also been very active to prevent rebel penetration from Syria to Lebanon, being one of the most active forces in the Syrian War spillover in Lebanon.

Hezbollah is the main Lebanese national resistance group loyal to defending Lebanon from an Israeli attack on Lebanon. It boasts a sophisticated fighting force and even controls key seats in Lebanon's parliament. Hezbollah maintains a vast social-services network throughout Lebanon that would be the envy of some small nation-states.

Led by Sayyed Hassan Nasrallah, Hezbollah has long maintained ties to Syria. For Syria was both a conduit through which Iran transferred weapons to Hezbollah and a place where some of its most influential leaders resided. Hezbollah has experienced mission creep in Syria, especially as circumstances have worsened for the Assad regime in the nascent stages of the conflict.

From an advice and assist type of role, Hezbollah fighters progressed to direct training of Syrian militias and full-fledged combat—including a ground offensive in April 2013 in Qusayr in the Homs province. Again, Hezbollah helped the Assad regime retake Aleppo.

So why has Hezbollah sent its members to fight and die in Syria, and what has it gained? Hezbollah has gained critical experience fighting in dense urban environments as well as familiarity

---

[22] **The *first zone*, covering Idlib province, also includes the north-eastern regions of Latakia, the western provinces of Aleppo and the northern regions of Hama province. More than a million civilians live in this zone.**

The *second zone* extends to the Rastan and Talbiseh enclave in the northern part of Homs province. About 180,000 civilians live in this zone.

The *third zone* is the most problematic to date; the zone is located in the northern suburbs of Damascus in Eastern Ghouta. About 700,000 civilians live here.

Last but not least, *the fourth zone* includes the provinces of Daraa and Quneitra in the south near the Syrian border with Jordan. The number of civilians here is close to 800,000 people.

According to the Astana agreements, both government forces and insurgents had to stop all hostilities in these territories, including air strikes, for six months. These zones should be surrounded by security buffers, as well as observation posts of the guarantor responsible for a certain zone. Finally, the zones should receive precise and unhindered deliveries of humanitarian aid.

Except for the third zone which covers Eastern Ghouta, these decisions managed to restore relative calm in the remaining three zones. According to the collective statement of the foreign ministers published following the March 16 Astana meeting, *all four de-escalation zones* will continue to operate. The zones were due to stop operating by the end of 2017, but the Russian Foreign Minister Sergey Lavrov stressed that the zones could continue to operate depending on the situation on the ground.

with fighting against enemies much different from its long-time foe, the Israel Defense Forces. In Syria, the Syrian militia refined its capabilities in battle against the Islamic State (ISIS). Hezbollah has perhaps been partly motivated to join the fight in Syria to counter the entrenched influence of Salafi-jihadist groups across the region, as well as their growing popularity within Lebanon. Indeed, pivoting from the group's stated justification for countering Israel. Nasrallah has identified fighting the Islamic State as one of the chief reasons for Hezbollah's involvement in Syria.

Hezbollah will also benefit from the enlarged alliance with Syria to one that now includes Russia (the Iran-Syria-Hezbollah relationship has been referred to as "Eastern Axis"). Indeed, U.S. officials have verified reports that Hezbollah militants have been working on the ground in tandem with not only Iranian Revolutionary Guards Corps Quds Force commanders, but also with Russian special operation troops, which is to Hezbollah a relaxing development. As a fighting force, Hezbollah's participation in these combined operations have likely helped improve the group's interoperability with other military organizations, improve its tactics, and expand its ability to command and control forces in a combat environment—all of which can be exported back in support to its native Lebanon.

When the Saudi cut off promised aid to Lebanon, it further the opening of the door for the Iranians to consolidate their influence on an east-west axis across Iraq, Syria and Lebanon, which was much more difficult when Iraq was a dedicated enemy. The conflict has taken on elements of a proxy war and now colors every aspect of the Saudi-Iranian relationships—religious, geopolitical and economic.

Who is the Free Syrian Army?

The Free Syrian Army (FSA) is supposed to be a faction in the Syrian War. It was founded on 29 July 2011 by few officers who defected from the Syrian Armed Forces and said their goal was to bring down the government of Bashar al-Assad.

FSA have said that the vast majority of its weaponry has been bought on the black market or seized from government facilities as they act as "rebel" groups who have captured a number of military bases since 2011 providing useful sources of ammunition and weapons, particularly anti-aircraft missile systems and armored vehicles.

But the truth is that Qatar was and is the main supplier of weapons to the "rebels" as well as the Gulf emirate has promised to support the opposition "with whatever it needs".

Most of the weapons have been given to the Islamist rebel groups, aligned with the Muslim Brotherhood. Qatar Emiri Air Force transporter planes flew to Turkey with supplies for the "Syria rebels" as early as January 2012, according to the New York Times, and by autumn 2012, Qatari aircraft were landing at Esenboga airport, near Ankara, every two days. While Qatari officials insisted, they were carrying non-lethal aid.

In turn, Saudi Arabia has taken the lead in channeling financial and military support to the "rebels" or ISIS.

In late 2012, Riyadh is said to have financed the purchase of "thousands of rifles and hundreds of machine guns", rocket and grenade launchers and ammunition for the FSA from a Croatian-controlled stockpile of Yugoslav weapons flown by Royal Saudi Air Force C-130 transporters - to Jordan and Turkey and smuggled into Syria.

Libya has been a key source of weapons for the FSA rebels and then ISIS. The UN Security

Council's Group of Experts, which monitors the arms embargo imposed on Libya during the 2011 uprising, said in April 2013 that there had been illicit transfers of *"heavy and light weapons, including man-portable air defense systems, small arms and related ammunition and explosives and mines"*. The significant size of some shipments and the logistics involved suggest that representatives of the Libyan local authorities might have at least been aware of the transfers, if not actually directly involved.

In May 2011, the European Union imposed an arms embargo on Syria. As the uprising entered its third year, several member states - led by the UK and France - lobbied to be able to supply arms to *"moderate"* forces in the opposition. Despite deep rifts, foreign ministers agreed to let the embargo lapse in May 2013. Though EU member states do not appear to have already sent arms directly to the rebels, another European country has been linked to a secret, large-scale airlift. In January 2013, a British blogger began to notice weapons made in the former Yugoslavia were appearing in videos and images posted online by "FSA rebels" fighting in southern Syria.

The recoilless guns, assault rifles, grenade launchers and shoulder-fired rockets appeared to be from an undeclared surplus from the 1990s Balkan wars stockpiled by Croatia.

It was reported that Western officials told the New York Times that the weaponry had been sold to Saudi Arabia, and that multiple planeloads had left Croatia since December 2012, bound for Turkey and Jordan. They were reportedly then given to several Western-aligned FSA groups.

The US has repeatedly said it is reluctant to supply arms directly to FSA rebel groups because it is concerned that weapons might end up in the possession of ISIS and militant jihadist groups.

But on 14 June 2013 Washington said it would give the FSA rebels "direct military aid" after falsely concluding and pretending that Syrian troops had used "chemical weapons".

The CIA is reported to have played an important role behind the scenes since 2012, co-coordinating arms shipments to the "rebels" by US allies.

In June 2012, US officials said CIA officers were operating in Turkey, helping decide which groups would receive weapons. The CIA is also reported to have been instrumental in setting up the alleged secret airlift of weapons from Croatia.

While the Turkish government is in reality a firm supporter of the Islamist groups "rebels", officially approved the sending of military aid; Turkey has played a pivotal role in sharp acceleration of arms shipments to the rebels since late 2012.

The Turkish authorities had oversight over much of the airlift of weapons from Croatia, *"down to affixing transponders to trucks ferrying the military goods through Turkey so it might be monitoring shipments as they move by land into Syria"*, according to the New York Times reports.

The Yugoslav-made weapons first seen in the hands of FSA units in southern Syria in early 2013 are believed to have been smuggled over the border with Jordan. However, the New York Times found evidence to suggest Royal Jordanian Air Force transport planes and Jordanian commercial aircraft had been involved in the alleged airlift of arms from Croatia.

Syria's rebels, who are drawn mostly from the country's majority Sunni community, are said to have acquired weapons, ammunition and explosives from Sunni tribesmen and militants in neighboring Iraq. Arms are reportedly smuggled over the long, porous border and sold or given to the "rebels". Al-Qaeda in Iraq played an active role in founding the al-Nusra Front and provides it with money, expertise and fighters.

As with Iraq, Lebanon's Sunni community is reported to have helped supply Syrian rebel fighters with small arms purchased on the black market or shipped from other countries in the region, including Libya. The Lebanese authorities have seized unmarked shipments of ammunition, including rocket-propelled grenades.

The Syrian town of Qusayr, which was recaptured by government forces in June 2013, was a transit point for weapons smuggled from north-eastern Lebanon.

Abundance of evidence exists to that money and arms intended for the shadowy "moderate" Islamists of the Free Syrian Army are filling the coffers and arsenals of the Nusra Front, although it is classified as a terrorist organization by the US and its allies.

The Causes for the Rise and Fall of ISIS in Iraq and Syria

The extreme jihadists are now mainly drawn to the so-called caliphate of ISIS, also known as Daesh. Several books have already charted the rise of "ISIS" out of the chaos of the 2003 US-led invasion of Iraq as the Islamic State; ISIS has stunned the world with its savagery, destructiveness, and military and recruiting successes. What explains the rise of ISIS is provided by Professor Gerges book[23] where a clear and compelling explanation of the deeper conditions that fuel ISIS exacerbated or increased the severity, bitterness and violence by foreign intervention, led to the rise and growth of ISIS.

I believe that by destroying state institutions and establishing a sectarian-based political system, the 2003 US-led invasion polarized the country along Sunni-Shia lines and set the stage for a fierce, prolonged struggle driven by identity politics with direct consequence of the sectarian feelings the invasion unleashed, for which America must bear responsibility.

Anger against the United States was also fueled by the humiliating disbandment of the Iraqi army and the de-Baathification law, which was first introduced as a provision and then turned into a permanent article of the constitution.

For example, Professor Gerges shows how the US de-Baathification program, combined with the growing authoritarianism and exclusion of Sunnis under Prime Minister Nuri al Maliki, provided fertile conditions for the emerging of ISIS out of al-Qaeda under the brutal leadership of Abu Musab al-Zarqawi and the self-styled caliph late Abu Bakr al-Baghdadi, his even more extreme successor. Al-Baghdadi was an evident fraud whose claim to legitimacy by virtue of his vicious genealogical grounds as descent from the Prophet's tribe.

De-Baathification was based on the American envoy Paul Bremer who deprived Iraq of its army and the administrative cadres that had ruled under Saddam Hussein, leaving the field to sectarian-based militias. Some 30 percent of the senior figures in ISIS's military command are former army and police officers from the disbanded Iraqi security forces. It was the military expertise of these men that transformed the Sunni-based insurgent movement of al-Qaeda in Iraq into ISIS, and became an effective fighting machine, combining urban guerilla warfare and conventional combat to deadly effect.

Al-Qaeda or Salafist-jihadist ideology became, by default, the identity chosen by many Sunnis facing Iranian-dominated Shia regimes—as they saw it—in Baghdad and Damascus, and a Kurdish revival in the north. These default identities should not be equated with religious fervor or commitment: rather that Iraq, like other postcolonial states in the Arab world, has nourished traditional institutions at the expense of a nationalist project around which citizens could unite….

---

[23] **Fawaz A. Gerges, "ISIS: A History", Princeton University Press, April 2016**

Sunnis and Shias feel entrapped in narrow communal identities and battles over identity rage not only between communities but within them.

The Destiny of Al-Qaeda in Iraq

Al-Qaeda in Iraq first appeared in 2004 when Abu Mus'ab al-Zarqawi, a Jordanian-born militant/terrorist already leading insurgent attacks in Iraq, formed an alliance with al-Qaeda, pledging his group's allegiance to Osama bin Laden in return for bin Laden's endorsement as the leader of al-Qaeda's franchise in Iraq. Al-Zarqawi, who quickly came to be regarded as one of the most destructive militants in Iraq, organized a wave of attacks, often suicide bombings that targeted security forces, government institutions, and Iraqi civilians. Intending to deepen the sectarian conflict at the heart of the Iraq War, al-Qaeda in Iraq especially targeted Iraqi Shiites, sometimes during religious processions or at Shiite mosques and shrines. A 2006 attack widely attributed to al-Qaeda in Iraq destroyed the golden dome of Al-Askariyyah Mosque in Samarra, one of Shiites holiest mosques, amplifying the existing cycle of violent retribution and provoking some of the worst sectarian violence of the post-invasion period.

Al-Qaeda in Iraq remained active even after al-Zarqawi was killed by U.S. forces in 2006. The organization was severely weakened in 2007; however, after Sunni tribes paid by the United States began to form militias known as "Awakening Councils" to expel al-Qaeda in Iraq from their territories. Many of those groups had previously participated in the insurgency but were alienated by al-Qaeda in Iraq's often brutal treatment of civilians, as well as its efforts to replace local tribal power structures with an al-Qaeda-governed state. Although that reversal, coupled with an increasingly successful effort by U.S. and Iraqi forces to kill al-Qaeda in Iraq leaders, greatly diminished the organization's power, the network continued to operate on a reduced scale, targeting Shiites, Christians, members of the Awakening Councils, and the Iraqi government.

Since most of the tanks in the city of Mosul were being used by Iraqi forces in the Anbar Province, the city was left with little to combat the ISIL fighters. On 4 June 2014, ISIL convoys of pickup trucks, each truck carrying four fighters, entered Mosul by shooting at the city's checkpoints and brutally hanging, burning, and crucifying some Iraqi soldiers during their attack.

ISIL continued with their attack on the northwestern part of the city on 6 June. The ISIL forces in the city totaled 1,500 terrorists, outnumbered by Iraqi forces by more than 15 to 1.

On 8 June, about a hundred vehicles entered Mosul, carrying at least four hundred men. Sleeper cells hidden within the city were activated.

On 9 June, ISIL terrorists executed fifteen Iraqi security force members who were captured in Tikrit; as they were armed with machine guns and rocket-propelled grenades stormed the Nineveh provincial headquarters that same day.

Lacking plans and ammunition, the Iraqi military retreated. On that same night, ISIL and Sunni militants attacked Mosul, causing heavy fighting overnight. Iraqi Army soldiers fled the city while it was under attack, allowing ISIL to control much of Mosul by midday on 10 June they seized numerous facilities, including Mosul International Airport, which had served as a hub for the U.S. military in the region. They captured the helicopters present at the airport, in addition to "several villages" and a military airbase in south Saladin Province.

The Iraqi army "crumbled in the face of the ISIL assault", which is evidenced by the fact reported that soldiers abandoned their weapons and dressed as civilians to blend in with the noncombatants.

The city fell to the ISIL on 10 June 2014 after four days of clashes between ISIL and the Iraqi military. There were reports that ISIL was advancing from Mosul to Kirkuk at the time. While capturing the city, the group freed nearly 1,000 prisoners, some of whom were greeted by the fighters. It was reported that the ISIL terrorists had captured a large part of Iraqi military equipment and supplies and also seized around $500 million in cash from Mosul Central Bank.

On 11 June, ISIL terrorists entered the oil refinery town of Baiji, seizing and setting its main courthouse and police station on fire.

The terrorist-militants, who were travelling in a group of around 60 vehicles, also took control of the Baiji prison and freed all the inmates within. Local residents told members of the media that ISIL sent a group of local tribal chiefs ahead of them, trying to convince the 250 guards at the oil plant to withdraw. Soldiers and police were also warned to leave the area. That day, ISIL terrorists also seized the Turkish consulate in Mosul, kidnapping 49 Turkish employees, including the Consul General, three children, and several members of the Turkish Special Forces. After seizing control of Mosul, ISIL terrorists executed an estimated 4,000 Iraqi Security Force prisoners and dumped their bodies in the single largest known mass grave in Iraq, at the "Khafsa Sinkhole."

In response to the Fall of Mosul and its aftermath, the Iraqi government said that it would arm its civilians and its parliament would declare a state of emergency. The government also spoke of a plan to reorganize its military, involving collaboration between tribal people and the U.S. military to recapture Mosul.

Iraqi forces initiated an offensive on October 17, 2016 to retake the city, succeeding in their efforts by mid-July 2017. The capture of Mosul was just not a big blow to Iraq but also a coup for the terror group's propaganda to establish an Islamic caliphate.

The re-capture of the city by Iraqi forces would mean an end to ISIS' strategic stronghold in Iraq. Moreover, the loss of Mosul would cut-off the route for its terrorists from its "de-facto capital" of Raqqa is Syria.

The Destiny of Al-Qaeda/al-Nusra in Syria

The Syrian branch of al Qaeda has undergone substantial changes over its presence in Syria. In mid-2016, the group announced it would no longer be known as Jabhat al-Nusra (Nusra Front) and would instead adopt the name Jabhat Fateh al-Sham (JFS) as part of the effort to distance itself from the al Qaeda network, signaling that they were truly independent of the international al Qaeda leadership, as well as to become feasible for the Sunni states in the Gulf to provide the militants with desperately needed resources to continue the fight against Syrian President Bashar al-Assad and his allies. It hoped to adopt a lower profile and elude the intense scrutiny the Islamic State (ISIS) receives from the Syrian regime, Russia and the United States. And while the United States places top priority on defeating ISIS, the al Qaeda-affiliated extremist groups that are consolidating territory around Idlib province in northwestern Syria have become targets of American airstrikes as well.

Al-Qaeda may have one possible motivation for the name change is that in Syria it believes its rival, ISIS, is headed toward defeat and that without ISIS to worry about. Al Qaeda had eschewed active intervention in many countries during the Arab Spring, and its leadership saw Syria as a chance to reestablish its relevance. Al Qaeda strategy on Syria seemed to do nothing to slow down its operations tempo of conducting attacks.

If terrorist groups linked to al Qaeda in Syria can succeed in rebranding themselves, they believe that they can take steps toward positioning themselves as political players if or when negotiations to end the war in Syria gain grip.

The Destiny of Al-Qaeda in Maghreb which encompasses Algeria, Libya, Mauritania, Morocco and Tunisia

In Tunisia:

In 1956, Tunisia's first post-independence leader, President Habib Bourguiba took power. He was a radical secularist; he imposed a modernizing agenda, including women's rights and Western-style education, while ruthlessly suppressing the forces of traditional religion. Even today one rarely sees men or women in traditional Islamic clothing in Tunis and many other parts of the country — a striking contrast to neighboring Libya, where *hijab*-wearing women are a common sight.

Pushing traditional religion to the side doesn't mean that everyone is going to agree; aggressive modernization almost always incites a backlash — and so it has gone in Tunisia, where those with an inclination to traditional Islam have often ended up feeling marginalized in their own country.

Tunisia is considered the cradle of the ill-fated Arab Spring. Tunisia remains the freest Arab democracy. It has one of the region's most developed economies and highest literacy rates. And it is also by far the largest source of foreign fighters headed and joined the Islamic State in Syria and Iraq (ISIS) with as many as 7,000 — more than twice the total from any other nation — having traveled to join the terrorist group's purported "caliphate" in Syria and Iraq.

The Tunisia revolution in 2011 brought an explosion of freedom of expression and political activity that extremists exploited after toppling Tunisian President Zine El Abidine Ben Ali. It was reported that under Ben Ali, people were banned from even praying. Religious books were confiscated, and lots of Islamic people — not just extremists — were arrested and jailed. Transformation to religious fundamentalist and ultimately foreign jihadist occurred after the 2011 revolution.

The collapse of the dictatorship in the 2011 revolution and the establishment of democratic institutions that followed had given jihadists new freedom to organize, travel, and share information. Religious radicals openly watch Salafist satellite broadcasts of hardline clerics streamed in from the Gulf and Egypt.

The moderate Islamist political party "Ennahda", the Muslim Brotherhood affiliate, long-banned by the Ben Ali regime, won the nation's first democratic election. But as a political and security crisis mounted anew in Tunisia in 2014, the party was pushed from power by popular vote. Followed by a period many Tunisians now say coincided with a wave of jihadist recruitment that the government made little effort to stop.

Rachid al-Ghannouchi, leader of Ennahda, made way for secular leaders after losing the struggle to have sharia written into the constitution. This offered the rare example of an Arab state system capable of embracing change. But the prospects everywhere else seem bleaker than ever, as the clans and tribal affiliated strive to maintain their grip on power.

Tunisians constitute the single largest group of foreign terrorist fighters in Syria, Iraq and Libya. They left Tunisia for the Islamic State's theocratic Salafist fanatic pseudo-state that has been consumed by violent extremism, war and resurgent authoritarianism.

As the Islamic State went on the defensive and lost the occupied territory in its Syrian and Iraqi strongholds. There are also places — including Tunisia — where jihadist movements remain very much on the offensive.

Tunisian officials, analysts and ordinary citizens say their nation is on a knife's edge, setting a precedent for freedom in the Arab world while scrambling to establish a post-dictatorship security state that can contain the threat of attacks by hardened Islamic State fighters who have returned — all without falling back into traditional patterns of authoritarian rule.

The fact that Tunisians have been dominated by strongly secularizing regimes for the past 61 years might well help to explain why democracy has taken root with such surprising success since 2011. But it also seems clear that that same modernizing trend has fueled an intense backlash among traditionalist Muslims, often to radical effect.

The fate of Tunisia, and its much-lauded democracy, will now depend on how well the country can figure out how to bridge the gap from becoming a prized target for the Islamic State and other Islamic extremists.

Tunisia has begun building a security wall along its own hundred-and-four-mile-long border with Libya. Do building walls secure safety or bring justice and democracy to any walled country?

In Libya:

Libya was a source of stability in the region under the leadership of Muammar Qaddafi who ruled in his fifth decade in office. In February, 2011, after a short, thrilling uprising inspired by the ouster of Hosni Mubarak, in Egypt, Libyan rebels based in Benghazi ousted Qaddafi's security forces and effectively liberated the eastern half of the country.

In March, as Qaddafi's military forces appeared poised to retake Benghazi, NATO intervened with air strikes and Tomahawk missiles. The U.N. authorized the intervention after British Prime Minister David Cameron and French President Nicolas Sarkozy lobbied in favor of it on humanitarian grounds; after showing some reserve, President Obama agreed to commit U.S. military power.

On October 20th, 2011, NATO air strikes destroyed a road convoy carrying Qaddafi in his home town of Sirte. He was captured by the rebels, who tortured and killed him. Most Libyans assumed that their moment of emancipation had come, but, as they grappled with their country's lack of institutions and a surplus of armed militias, they faltered and ultimately failed to find the path to democracy that Cameron and Sarkozy had promised.

David Cameron's special envoy for Libya, Jonathan Powell, acknowledged that the West bore some responsibility for Libya's collapse acknowledging that the West *"made a mistake leaving Libya so soon after Qaddafi's downfall"*.

Battle-hardened Libyan Islamists, who had returned home from fighting in Iraq and Syria, along with Islamists from other countries, seized the eastern city of Derna and claimed it for ISIS. Emulating their comrades in Raqqa and Mosul, they stoned, shot, beheaded, and crucified people deemed guilty of espionage or "un-Islamic" behavior.

ISIS advanced amid a low-level war, pitting militias and tribes against one another in alliances that defy easy description. Libya's displaced government—which is based in the east, while a militia-backed government holds sway in Tripoli—carried out air strikes against two ships off the eastern coast, sinking one that allegedly carried jihadists and weapons.

Benghazi became a war zone, where militias loyal to both governments, as well as jihadists, battle daily. Large swatches of the city have been destroyed, and hundreds of civilians have died in the fighting.

There is also a regional-proxy-war element to consider. The eastern government in Benghazi is backed by Egypt's military regime, Saudi Arabia, and the United Arab Emirates; while the Tripoli coalition is connected to the Muslim Brotherhood and backed by Turkey and Qatar.

A tentative peace agreement that called for a ceasefire, between Libya's rival governments, a timetable for new elections, and the deployment of international peacekeeping troops. The agreement was signed by the eastern government and by city councils and civil-society leaders, but not, crucially, by the hard-liners within the Islamist militia coalition that holds power in Tripoli, nor by Khalifa Heftar, a former army general who leads the anti-Islamist forces that are fighting in the east.

A note to remember that Qaddafi warned that Al Qaeda and other Islamic extremists would capitalize on the uprising against him. Libya, he warned, would be dismembered. In light of what has happened since, it seems safe to say that Qaddafi was right.

Libya's Islamic State militant group, such as (ISIS), is by now perceived widely as a major threat in North Africa and the southern Mediterranean. The political chaos in Libya certainly has provided the opportunity for any Islamic State (IS) to flourish. But that was not possible without two major factors: The increasing willingness of Libyan regions that lost power in the post-revolutionary era to support an Islamic State and the availability of a steady stream of jihadi terrorists from neighboring Tunisia.

In Algeria:

Algeria won its independence from France in 1962 after bloody eight-year war led by the National Liberation Front (NLF). After independence, NLF ruled Algeria for 30 years. Although it enjoyed considerable prestige based on this success, it squandered its popular support by building a one-party socialist state that badly mismanaged Algeria's deepening economic, social, and political problems.

The NLF nationalized large portions of the economy and built a Soviet-style command economy. It undertook an overly ambitious industrialization program that led to the development of swollen, inefficient state enterprises. The mismanaged socialist economy was kept afloat by Algeria's oil and gas revenues, but the 1985-1986 falls in energy prices dealt a body blow to the economy, reducing oil revenues from $12.5 billion in 1985 to $8 billion in 1986.[24] Rather than institute free-market economic reforms to revive the economy, the NLF regime borrowed heavily abroad.

Algerians grew profoundly disenchanted with the NLF's one-party rule and its inability to deal with problems as high unemployment, chronic food shortages, overcrowded housing, rising prices, and an overburdened infrastructure.

In October 1988, anti-NLF riots swept many Algerian cities and the mass demonstrations subsequently took on an Islamist cast and spread from the capital to other cities.

The chief political challenge to the NLF came from the Islamic Salvation Front (FIS), a coalition of more than 20 Islamist groups dedicated to creating an Islamic state ruled by the Sharia, Islam's sacred law, was officially made legal as a political party in September 1989, less than a year later the FIS received more than half of valid votes cast by Algerians in the 1990 local government elections.

---

[24] **Paul Collier and Nicholas Sambanis, "Understand Civil War", Volume 1: Africa, the World Bank Publication, 2005, p. 224**

When it appeared to be winning a general election in January 1992, a military coup dismantled the party interning thousands of its officials in the Sahara. It was officially banned two months later.[25]

The Islamic State fanatics formally announced the start of operations in Algeria. Previously, Algeria's militants had been relatively quiet, beheading a single French tourist in September 2014 when a group of militants deserted al-Qaeda in the Islamic Maghreb and pledged allegiance to the Islamic State of (ISIS). The ISIS leadership has vowed to continue their attacks in Algeria and pledged to extend their operations against People National Army (PNA) forces. They have threatened to strike the whole North Africa, including the countries of Maghreb.

Algeria engulfed in a bloody war that has claimed around 40,000 lives since January 1992 when the Algerian army seized power, ousted President Chadli Benjedid, and canceled parliamentary elections to avert a takeover by Islamic radicals, or "Islamists."

The provisional military government and the loose coalition of Islamists who seek its overthrow have fought to a standstill. It is gradually becoming clear that neither side is likely to score a decisive military victory. Algeria disintegrated into political chaos that destabilized the entire region.

But as bad as Algeria's situation is, an Islamist victory would be even worse. The Islamic State of Iraq and al-Sham (ISIS) and al-Qaeda in the Islamic Maghreb (AQIM) are competing to be the dominant Salafi-jihadi group in Algeria, the Jaza'er Providence or (Wilayat el Jaza'ir). Wilayat Jaza'ir, ISIS's affiliate in Algeria, first gained a foothold in Algeria through the defection of small AQIM factions and pledges of support from groups previously associated with ISIS. Then it launched a campaign of ambushes and small explosive attacks targeting Algerian security forces in late 2015. It is recruiting by calling for the immediate overthrow of North African regimes.

Algeria suffered through a decade-long insurgency since the 1990s when jihadists returned from Afghanistan set on establishing Islamic law, and the army led a brutal war to crush them.

In Egypt:

In Egypt, dictator Hosni Mubarak was overthrown in 2011, and Mohammad Mosri Al Ayat, an Egyptian politician became the fifth President of Egypt, from 30 June 2012 to 3 July 2013.

As president, Morsi issued a temporary constitutional declaration in late November that in effect granted him unlimited powers and the power to legislate without judicial oversight or review of his acts.

The new constitution that was then hastily drawn up by the Islamist-dominated constitutional assembly, presented to the president, and scheduled for a referendum, before the Supreme Constitutional Court could rule on the constitutionality of the assembly, was described by independent press agencies not aligned with the regime as an "Islamist coup".

On 30 June 2013, protests erupted across Egypt, which saw protesters calling for the president's resignation. In response to the events, Morsi was given a 48-hour ultimatum by the military to meet their demands and to resolve political differences, or else they would intervene by *implementing their own road map*" for the country. The military coup d'état led by General Abdel Fattah el-Sisi removed Morsi from office and suspended the constitution and established a new administration.

The Muslim Brotherhood protested against the military coup, but the pro-Morsi protests were crushed in the August 2013 Rabaa massacre in which at least 817 civilians were killed. Brotherhood

---

[25] **Dalacoura, Katerina. "*Islamic Terrorism and Democracy in the Middle East*", Cambridge University Press. 2011, p. 106**

officials singled out the Christian Copts, and particularly Coptic Pope Tawadros, for being complicit in the General Sisi-led military coup, and Christians were the target of angry supporters.

In August 2013, Human Rights Watch reported that mob violence led by Brotherhood supporters damaged 42 churches and dozens of schools and businesses owned by Copts across Egypt, killing several and trapping Christians in their homes.

Islamist circles and some Muslims across Egypt, meanwhile, use rhetoric ridiculing Christians as a "favored class" that is "hoarding wealth" and benefits from the regime, fault-lines that ISIS was looking to exploit.

Since his overthrow, Egyptian prosecutors have charged Morsi with various crimes and sought the death penalty his death sentence was overturned, so he received a retrial.

By 2013, when Muslim Brotherhood President Mohammad Morsi was ousted as leader, the group had targeted the Egyptian security forces. In November 2014, Ansar Bait al-Maqdis (ABM), who grew out of militant Bedouin tribes operating in the Sinai, monopolizing smuggling networks, most likely over the Egyptian frontier into Gaza, pledged allegiance to the ISIS leader Abu Bakr al-Baghdadi, and became known as Sinai Province (Wilayat Sinaa').

Two years later, President Abdel Fattah el-Sisi led a military takeover promising to restore order and security in Egypt, he faces a rising jihadist insurgency that has shaken the stability of his country.

Conclusion:

The best way to strangle ISIS and the Nusra Front would be for Arabs to collectively resolve their spiraling sectarian conflicts and support state-building structures. The wishful thinking that flows from the false premise that Western powers can co-opt radical Muslim movements through negotiation, dialogue, and compromise practices valued in democratic societies but not in radical Islam.

CHAPTER FOUR
THE DESTABILIZATION OF SYRIA

The Syrian war turned to be a war by proxy that was planned in advance to secure the American dominance and the Zionist-Israeli influence in the Middle East. What is unfolding in Syria is an armed insurrection supported covertly by foreign powers including the US, Turkey and "Israel".

Members of the Muslim Brotherhood are reported to have taken up arms in northwest Syria, starting the year 2011. The center of the mutiny has started from a small border town of Jisr al-Shughour, of 44,000 inhabitants, 10 km from the Turkish border. Armed insurgents belonging to Islamist organizations have crossed the border from Turkey and Jordan; especially from Turkey military and intelligence are supporting these incursions.

According to Chossudovsky, [26] the demonstrations started in Daraa, a city of about 300,000, near the border with Jordan, was fast becoming a major challenge for President Bashar Assad, rather than in Damascus or Aleppo, where the mainstay of organized political opposition and social movements are located.

There was no mass civilian protest movement in Jisr al-Shughour. The local population was caught in the crossfire. The fighting between armed terrorist's "rebels" and government forces has contributed to triggering a refugee crisis, which became the center of media attention.

In the nation's capital Damascus, where the foundation of social movements is located, there have been mass rallies in support rather than in opposition to the government, where President Bashar al Assad was compared to presidents Ben Ali of Tunisia and Hosni Mubarak of Egypt, but the mainstream media has failed to mention that despite the authoritarian nature of the regime, President Al Assad is a popular figure who has widespread support of the Syrian population. The attempt to use the riots in Syria by the U.S. and the E.U. to pressure and intimidate the Syrian leadership for eight years did not succeed.

It is important to remember that the US State Department has confirmed that It was supporting the insurgency in Syria. The United States was to expand contacts with Syrians who were counting on a regime change in the country. This was stated by U.S. State Department official Victoria Nuland [27] as such: *"We started to expand contacts with the Syrians, those who are calling for change, both inside and outside the country,"* she also repeated that *"Barack Obama had previously called on Syrian President Bashar Assad to initiate reforms or to step down from power."*

No doubt that the destabilization of Syria and Lebanon as sovereign countries has been on the drawing board of the US-NATO-Israel military alliance for at least ten years.

Action against Syria was part of a "military roadmap", a sequencing of military operations. According to former NATO Commander General Wesley Clark, the Pentagon had clearly identified Iraq, Libya, Syria and Lebanon as target countries of a US-NATO intervention:

I would like to quote a paragraph from General Wesley Clark's book [28] where he wrote: "... *As I went back through the Pentagon in November 2001, one of the senior military staff officers had*

[26] **Chossudovsky, Michel, "SYRIA: Who is Behind the Protest Movement?" Fabricating a Pretext for a US-NATO Humanitarian Intervention, Global Research, May 3, 2011.**

[27] **Voice of Russia, June 17, 2011**

[28] **General Wesley Clark, "In Winning Modern Wars: Iraq, Terrorism and The American Empire",** **PublicAffairs; 1ˢᵗ US - 1ˢᵗ Printing edition (October 16, 2003),** *page 130*

time for a chat. Yes, we were still on track for going against Iraq, he said. But there was more. This was being discussed as part of a five-year campaign plan, he said, and there was a total of seven countries, beginning with Iraq, then Syria, Lebanon, Libya, Iran, Somalia and Sudan. He said it with reproach--with disbelief, almost--at the breadth of the vision. I moved the conversation away, for this was not something I wanted to hear. And it was not something I wanted to see moving forward, either. ...I left the Pentagon that afternoon deeply concerned."

The objective is to destabilize the Syrian State and implement *regime change* through the covert support of an armed insurgency, integrated by Islamist militia.

As the proxy war entered its seventh year, the country has been destroyed beyond repair. Even if the international community can cobble together a negotiated settlement that brought an end to the violence, overwhelming damage has been done. Since the war began in 2011, an estimated four hundred thousand Syrians have been killed, almost five million have fled the country and more than six million have been internally displaced. Most of Syria's major cities—including its former commercial hub Aleppo—have been reduced to rubble.

What Happened to the Syrian Arab Christian villages?

Maaloula is a Christian town with an Aramean population that speaks Aramaic, the language of Jesus Christ, and Arabic located in the Rif Dimashq Governorate in Syria. The town is located 56 km to the northeast of Damascus and built into the rugged mountainside, at an altitude of more than 1500 meters, was attacked by Jabhat al Nusra (the Nusra Front) Jihadits who had been based in the mountains near the Safir hotel since March 2013. It was reported that the jihadists were harassing the Christian people of the village since then. Maaloula was attacked in September 2013. The attackers torched a church and looted another one and threatened several Christian villagers with beheading if they did not convert to Islam as reported.[29]

During the proceeding weekend, twelve nuns from the Greek Orthodox monastery of Mar Takla were kidnapped and taken toward the border town of Yabroud. At the time the kidnappers claimed that they were not abducting the nuns. However, two months later the nuns were ransomed in exchange for government held prisoners.

On 14 April 2014, with the help of the Lebanese Freedom Fighters of Hezbollah and the Syrian Army took control of Maaloula. This success was part of a string of other successes in the strategic Qalamoun region, including the seizure of the former terrorist stronghold of Yabroud in the previous month.

Maaloula was not the only Christian town attacked. ISIS, the self-proclaimed Islamic State, also had launched a fierce offensive before dawn February 23, targeting 35 Assyrian Christian villages in the northeast corner of Syria. The surprise attacks along a 40-kilometer stretch of the Khabour River in Hassaka province forced some 3,000 Christians to flee their homes.

By looking at the geographical map of the Syrian Arab Republic with historic knowledge of the region, you find out that Syria Is a unitary state, but for administrative purposes, it is divided into fourteen governorates (muhafazat). The governorates are divided into sixty districts (manatiq), which are further divided into sub-districts (nawahi).

The concentration of Syrian Arab Christians towns from the ancient Assyrian ethnicity are mainly distributed in three governorates that of Hasaka, Damascus and Homs. Syria Arab Christians live in

---

[29] **The daily Star, *"Jihadists force Syria Christian to convert at gunpoint"*, September 11, 2013**

seven cities of Hassaka, in 11 villages, and 40 in the Khabour valley. Christians formed the majority in Syria's Jazeera area, which includes Hasaka governorate.

In the Damascus governorate, we have Arab Christians in the capital city of Damascus, as well as in the two old and famous Assyrian Aramaic towns of Maaloula and Saidnaya.

In Homs governorate, there are four Christian towns of Fairouzeh, Zaidal, Al-Qaryatain and Salad.

What Happened to the Syrian World Heritage Site and Historic Towns?

The Islamic State ISIS captured Palmyra, the "Pearl of the Desert," about 150 miles northeast of Damascus, in May 2015, and it quickly started targeting cultural sites and killing soldiers and some residents who had been left behind.

ISIS destroyed the facade of a second-century Roman theater and another ancient monument in the historic city of Palmyra, Syria, and severely damaged a tetrapyon, a square structure of four plinths, each with four columns. Only two columns are still standing of the tetrapylon, after being destroyed intentionally by using explosives. They destroyed ancient artifacts, including the 1,800-year-old Arch of Triumph, once a popular draw for tourists, and the nearly 2,000-year-old Temple of Baalshamin. Temples have stood in Palmyra for thousands of years.

The smashing of the ancient structures was a further attempt by ISIS to impose its will by destroying monuments or artifacts that it says do not conform to its strict interpretation of Islam.

ISIS terrorized citizens and destroyed numerous priceless remains in the desert city of Palmyra which was declared a World Heritage site by the United Nations Educational, Scientific and Cultural Organization (UNESCO). UNESCO has branded the actions "*cultural cleansing.*"

The targeting of Palmyra's cultural treasures has particular resonance as the city's heritage, which embodies Greek, Persian, Roman and Islamic cultures, is a vivid symbol of a prewar, multicultural Syria that is anathema to the Islamic State's brutal and monolithic worldview.

UNESCO World Heritage Convention was established in 1972. The Syrian Arab Republic accepted the convention on 13 August 1975, making its historical sites eligible for inclusion on the World historical heritage site list. As of 2016, six sites in Syria are officially included. The following bird's eye view about of each historic site and the year of admittance:

Ancient City of Damascus

Note that the ancient city of Damascus was established in the 3rd millennium BC, Damascus is considered to be one of the oldest continuously inhabited cities in the world. As the capital of the Ummayyads, it has been of significant influence to the Arab world. The Great Mosque is among the largest in the world and the oldest sites of continuous prayer since the beginnings of Islam.

Site of Palmyra

Palmyra came under Roman rule in the 1st century CD and grew to become one of the most important cultural centers of the ancient world. Its extensive ruins include remains of the Great

Colonnade, the Temple of Bel, the Camp of Diocletian (a Roman military complex), and the Roman theatre. And

Ancient City of Bosra

Formerly a Nabatanean settlement, Bosra was conquered by the Romans in the 2nd century CD and made capital of Arabia. It came under Islamic rule in the 7th century. Remains of the ancient city include a theatre, a basilica, a cathedral, a mosque and a madrasa, among others.

Ancient City of Aleppo

The ancient city of Aleppo is situated at the crossroads of several trade routes. Aleppo has been successively ruled, among others, by the Romans, Ayyubids, Mameluks and Ottomans, each leaving significant influence in its architectural fabric, resulting in a diverse cityscape. Major structures include the Cital, the Great Mosque, and the Madrasa Halawiye.

Crac des Chevaliers and Qal'at Salah El-Din (2006)

The Crac des Chevaliers and the Qal'at Salah El-Din are regarded as two of the most prominent examples of castles during the Crusader period, demonstrating an evolution of fortifications and exchange of influences in defensive technology.

Ancient Villages of Northern Syria

The site comprises some 40 villages, dating from the 1st to 7th centuries and abandoned in the 8th to 10th centuries. They provide an insight into rural life in Late Antiquity and during the Byzantine.

The List of Tentative Sites in Syria

Syria has also a list of tentative sites that they may consider for nomination. Nominations for the World Heritage list are only accepted if the site was previously listed on the tentative list. As of 2016, Most of the information of the listed twelve sites on the Syrian tentative list are taken from the Ancient History Encyclopedia. These sites are the followings:

- *Norias of Hama* ((نواعير حماة)

The giant and magnificent waterwheels, the Norias of Hama, were submitted as a tentative World Heritage Site by the Syrian Arab Republic in June 1999.

Each of the wheels is close to 70 feet and the water is channeled in to a dip on the wheel. This flow then forces the wheel to turn and wood boxes raise the water upwards. At the top of the wheel there is an artificial channel in which the water is discharged. The largest has 120 water collectors and was capable of delivering almost one hundred liters of water each minute to the aqueduct. Although none of the larger norias are now in use they are being maintained by the Syrian government so that future generations can witness the ingenuity of centuries gone by them.

- ### *The City of Ugarit at Tell Ras Shamra*

The Ugarit Tell Ras Shamra was a Kingdom on the Mediterranean coast, flourished during the 2nd millennium B.C.

The current city of Ugarit is some 11 kilometers (7 mi) north of Latikia. Various excavations, which began in 1929, cover only one-sixth of this vast site. This work uncovered quarters of some capital, temples, and remains of a fortification, a large royal palace, and numerous houses. Other discoveries – including archive tablets and numerous archaeological objects – are of exceptional and universal importance.

- ### *Elba (Tell Mardikh)*

Ebla, modern Tall Mardīkh, is ancient city 33 miles (53 km) southwest of Aleppo in northwestern Syria in current Idlib Governorate. Ebla is one of the most extensive archaeological sites from the Bronze Age in western Syria.

During the height of its power (2600–2240 B.C), Ebla dominated northern Syria, Lebanon, and parts of northern Mesopotamia (modern Iraq), and enjoyed trade and diplomatic relations with states as far away as Egypt and Iran.

Excavation of the Tall or tell (mound) now known to be the site of Ebla started in 1964 with a team of archaeologists from the University of Rome led by Paolo Matthiae. In 1975 Matthiae's team found Ebla's archives, dating to the 3rd millennium B.C. Discovered virtually intact in the order in which they had once been stored on their now-collapsed shelves were more than 17,000 clay cuneiform tablets and fragments, offering a rich source of information about Ebla.

- ### *Mari (Tell Hariri)*

Mari was an ancient Semitic city in Syria. Its remains constitute a tell located 11 kilometers north-west of Abu Kamal on the Euphrates river western bank, some 120 kilometers southeast of Deir ez-Zor. The ruins of Mari are located at modern-day *Tell Hariri* in eastern Syria.

During the Early Bronze Age and the Middle Bronze Age, Mari was one of the earliest known planned cities. Mari is believed to have been founded as a trade hub, and copper and bronze-smelting center, between Babylonia in Southern Mesopotamia and the resource-rich Taurus Mountains of modern Turkey. For 1,200 years, Mari served as a major center of Northern Mesopotamia until it was destroyed by Hammurabi of Babylon between 1760 BC and 1757 BC and gradually eroded away from memory and quite literally - today only one-third of the city survives with the rest washed away by the Euphrates.

Mari is an early example of complex urban planning and is believed to have been entirely planned out prior to its actual construction by another unknown but complex society. This is evident in Mari's overall design as the city was built as two concentric rings, the outer ring intended to protect the city from the occasional violent floods of the Euphrates, and the inner ring designed to defend against attackers.

• Dura-Europos

Dura Europos was founded in 303 BC by the Seleucids (Alexander the Great's successors) on the intersection of an east-west trade route and a north-south trade route along the Euphrates. The new city, named for the birthplace of Seleucus I Nicator, controlled the river crossing on the route between Antioch on the Orontes and Seleucia on the Tigris. Dura Europos was part of a network of military colonies intended to secure Seleucid control of the Middle Euphrates.

Dura Europos later became a frontier fortress of the Parthian Empire and it was captured by the Romans in 165 AD. In the early 200s AD, the famed house-church and synagogue were built at Dura Europos. It is an ancient synagogue uncovered at Dura-Europos, near the village of Salhiya, in Syria, in 1932. The last phase of construction was dated by an Aramaic inscription to 244 AD making it one of the oldest synagogues in the world.

The Excavations at Dura-Europos was conducted by Yale University and the French Academy of Inscriptions and Letters.[30]

• Apamea or Afamia (Qalaat al-Mudik) آفامیا

The city of Apamea or Afamia was founded in 301 B.C. It is one of the most important cities of North Syria in the Seleucid era. At the beginning of the Roman era, Afamia counted some 117,000 inhabitants. Due to its strategic position at that time, it played both a prominent military and commercial role.

Afamia is an ancient city located on the right bank of the Orontes River about 55 km northwest of Hama, Syria. It overlooks the Ghab valley and is notable for its exceptionally long Roman Street, lined with classical columns.

The Afamia site is considered to be one of the most affected sites as a result of ongoing illegal excavations, which are centered on the eastern, north-eastern, and western regions of the city.

• Deser Castle: Qasr al-Hayr al-Sharqi

The Eastern Castle has been preserved and in part reconstructed in place. The complex is composed of two main buildings (called large enclosure and small enclosure) and a bathhouse. The large enclosure has an outer structure of stone and reinforced with twenty-eight towers and four entrance gates, one for each facade.

The outer enclosure is also built in stone and coated inside with clay brick built on stone foundations. Close to the main building is a bathhouse which includes a large hall 20 by 15 meters with two pools fed by water tanks, completed by changing rooms (one for the summer and one for winter) and latrines. There were also three hot rooms located near the heat source and service areas including water tanks.

Qasr al-Hayr al-Sharqi was excavated in six seasons between 1964 and 1971 by an American

---

[30] **Kraeling C. H. (With contributions by Torrey C. C., Welles C. B., and Geiger B.), "Final Report VIII. Part I. The Synagogue," Yale University Press, New Haven, and Oxford University Press, London, 1956**

team led by Oleg Grabar [31]. Since then, a Syrian team has conducted excavation and restoration work. Most of the decorations of the façade have been relocated to the National Museum of Damascus.

- ### *Maaloula*

The city of Maaloula and its surroundings towns Bakh'a and Jubba'din are classified as a cultural site in the Tentative List of UNESCO since August 6, 1999. Maaloula and the nearby towns of Bakh'a and Jubba'din are the last places in the world where the Aramaic language is still spoken. They are outstanding of historical, religious and cultural heritage. -The city is built being adapted to the natural shape of the territory, composing a mixed landscape that shows the interaction between human being and nature.

Maaloula is 50 kilometers from Damascus, at an altitude of more than 1500 meters, in the direction of Lebanon. Maaloula rests on the slopes of the Kalamun Mountains as if it were in reality a gigantic bee-hive on the edge of a rock face.

There are two important monasteries in Maaloula: Greek Catholic Mar Sarkis and Greek Orthodox Mar Takla. There are also the remains of numerous monasteries, convents, churches, shrines and sanctuaries. There are some that lie in ruins, while others continue to stand, defying age.

- ### *Island of Arwad* أرواد

The Island of Arwad in Syria is 49 acres and is located in the eastern coast of the Mediterranean Sea and is the only inhabited town that covers the entire island.

Not much more than a dot of rock off the coast of Tartous, Syria, Arwad once dominated a goodly stretch of that coast, ruling the mainland like an offshore castle. History records that war galleys of Arwad fought on the side of the Egyptians, the Assyrians and even the Persians when the tide turned for Greece in the early fifth century BC. More than a millennium and a half later, the island became the last bastion in the entire Levant for the crusading Knights Templar [32] before their final, dramatic expulsion. Though Arwad today is a quieter place, the remains of its massive stone fortifications have many a tale to tell.

The island was once insulated also by a massive outer city wall made of gargantuan stone blocks. As historian Lawrence Conrad [33] describes it, in Byzantine times *"the great walls surrounding the island on all but the harbor side were at least 10 meters high in places and were built of tremendous*

---

[31] **Oleg Grabar (November 3, 1929 – January 8, 2011) was a French-born art historian and Archeologist, who spent most of his career in the United States, as a leading figure in the field of Islamic art and architecture**

[32] **Around 1118 AD, a French knight named Hugues de Payens created a military order along with eight relatives and acquaintances, calling it the Poor Fellow-Soldiers of Christ and the Temple of Solomon—later known simply as the Knights Templar. The Knights Templar became a large organization of devout Christians with a mission: to protect European travelers visiting sites in the Holy Land while also carrying out military operations.**

[33] **Concard, Lawrence, *"The Conquest of Arwad: A Source-Critical Study in the Historiography of the Early Medieval Near East,"* Book Chapter, 1992**

blocks up to six meters long and two meters high." The walls, according to Conrad, dated at least to the Seleucid era that followed Alexander the Great, and probably even to the Phoenician era before.

• Tartous: The City-fortress of the Crusaders

Tartous was originally founded by the Phoenicians to complement the more secure but the less accessible settlement on the island of Arwad. For a longtime it served a secondary role to Arwad, itself a major center in Seleucid and Roman times.

Tartous underwent a major program of rebuilding in 346 A.D. under the Byzantine Emperor Constantine, probably because it housed an important ancient shrine dedicated to the Virgin Mary. It was for a while consequently renamed Constantia, although it soon reverted to its ancient name Tartous. It is under this name - or its Latinized form of Tortosa- that it became famous in Crusader times as one of the main Frankish littoral settlements in Syria, perhaps more importantly as the headquarters of the Templar knights.

In Christian hands the fortress was a very important and strategic outpost located close to *Nahr el-Kabir* or the 'Gate of Homs', a large gap in the formidable mountain ranges that stand behind the coastal strip and which allowed access to the valley of the Orontes River and to important towns of Homs and Hama.

Tartous Citadel (well-known now as the Old City of Tartous) remains today the only clear historical center, and its main architectural features belong to two periods: The Late Ottoman and the French Mandate (between the 19th century and the first half of the 20th century).

• Mari & Europos-Dura: Sites of Euphrates Valley

Mari & Europos-Dura sites of Euphrates Valley are part of the tentative list of Syria in order to qualify for inclusion in the World Heritage List. The two cities of Mari and Europos-Dura were founded on the western bank of Euphrates River. The cities were at a key location, where they controlled the route on the Euphrates that connected the Mediterranean world with Mesopotamia and greater Asia.

Mari is probably the archaeological reference site that has provided the greatest amount of information useful to understand the history between the Third and the end of the Second millennia in Syros-Mesopotamia.

Its situation between the two seas, the *"rising sun"* and the *"setting sun"*- the Persian/Arabian Gulf and the Mediterranean - made Mari an almost-obligatory passage point.

Mari played a key role for almost a millennium. It is the site of reference that makes it possible to understand the fundamental aspects of the Syros-Mesopotamian civilization of the Third millennium (early Bronze and Bronze ages). After 42 excavation campaigns, it is one of the best-known cities of the Middle Eastern Antiquity.

Mari featured a wealth of prestigious palaces and temples, and art schools where beautiful sculpture and painting works were produced, with an exceptional quantity of administrative archives dating back to the last periods of the city, during the time of the Hammurabi of Babylon; This data makes it possible to understand the economic life of this time and the management of the kingdom. Mari remains a particularly fertile area of research on the first great urban civilizations.

The development of the city of Mari was accompanied by the implementation of a monumental architecture, well anchored in the Mesopotamian constructive tradition. The greatness of the palaces, the temples and the residences conferred an exceptional character to the city.

Because it was founded around 2900 BC, just in the beginning of the expansion of urbanization, Mari allows the study of urban expansion in Mesopotamia, and the changes that occurred in the rapid evolution from a rural way of life to an urban way life, including all the changes related to economic, political and social organization. It is thus an exceptional resource to understand one of the crucial periods in the development of humanity, to which we are still deeply connected.

It is important that all necessary measures must be taken to protect and preserve the fragile architecture of Mari.

Europos-Dura represent another great archaeological find of historical and artistic interest. The very extensive site comprises Hellenistic and Roman ruins enclosed within massive city walls, being situated on the right bank of the middle course of the River Euphrates, about 90 kilometers along the road from Deir ez-Zor to the Abu-Kamal Bridge and the present-day border with Iraq.

Europos-Dura has been discovered in 1920, explored from Europos-Dura represent another great archaeological find of historical and artistic interest. The very extensive site comprises Hellenistic and Roman ruins enclosed within massive city walls, being situated on the right bank of the middle course of the River Euphrates, about 90 kilometers along the road from Deir ez-Zor to the Abu-Kamal Bridge and the present-day border with Iraq. Europos-Dura was founded around 303 B.C. as a stronghold with military function by the Seleucids on the route along the Euphrates.

The two sites represent the best-preserved remains of ancient times complete with its environment. This makes them a valuable component of Syria's cultural heritage well worth preserving. Mari and Europos-Dura display a mixture of influences which has created a unique architecture, culture and townscape, with exceptional buildings of Palaces, public and religious buildings of different faiths, with reflections on urbanism, fine arts, and based on a prosperous trading economy. Mari and Europos-Dura represent exceptional examples of trading cities in Mesopotamia, forged from the mercantile, religious and cultural exchanges of several civilizations (Sumerian, Greek, and Roman), with each culture having left its imprint on the built and living environment.

The remaining of Mari is still impressive in height and material (the mud brick construction can be easily appreciated). Currently a French and Syrian team is applying a mud plaster to the walls as a conservation measure, in an attempt to prevent further loss.

The conservation activities in Mari covering the safeguarding site of mud brick archaeological site play an essential part for the implementation of the recommendation of regional seminar on conservation of earthen structure in the Arab states held in Masqat on December 2003.

Also, the re-examination of Europos site is currently underway through the work of joint Franco-Syrian Expedition one of whose more urgent tasks is to stop the damage in the site. In Syria the comparison would be in the light of the political and historical situation in Mesopotamia in the 3rd and 2nd millennia BC, these come from a variety of geographical locations, including Ugarit, Ebla, and Mari as sites within Mesopotamia proper.

Witnessing the Battle of ar-Raqqah

The last tentative site on the list is ar-Raqqah which was in March 2013, during the Syrian War, overran by Islamist Jihadist terrorists from an-Nusra and other groups (including the Free Syrian

Army) in the Battle of ar-Raqqah and they declared it under their control after seizing the central square and pulling down the statue of the former president of Syria Hafez Al-Assad.

The Al-Qaeda affiliated Al-Nusra set up ash-Shari'a court at the sport center. In early June 2013 the Islamic State of Iraq and the Levant (ISIL) took complete control of Ar-Raqqah by 13 January 2014.

ISIL proceeded to execute Alawites and suspected supporters of the Syrian President Bashar Al-Assad in the city and destroyed the city's Shia mosques and Christian churches such as the Armenian Catholic Church of the Martyrs, which has since been converted into an ISIL headquarters. The Christian population of Al-Raqqah, which had been estimated to be more than 10% of the total population before the war began, were killed or fled the city. ISIL in ar-Raqqah will be defeated and the Syrian Arab Army with the help of his allies, Russia and Hezbollah, will liberate it and restore it to its inhabitants.

- ### *Raqqa-Rafiqah: The Abbasid City*

Ar-Raqqah الرقة is the sixth largest city in Syria. It is located on the northeast bank of the Euphrates River. The area of ar-Raqqah has been inhabited since remote antiquity. The modern city traces its history to the Hellenistic period, with the foundation of the city of Nikephorion by the Seleucid king Seleucus I Nicator who reigned from 301 to –281 BC. Seleleucus II Calinicus. 246–225 BC enlarged the city and renamed it after himself as Kallinikos.

In the 6th century, Kallinikos became a center of Assyrian monasticism. Dayr Maar Zakkaa, or the Saint Zaccaeus Monastery, situated on Tall al-Bi'a, became renowned. A mosaic inscription there is dated to the year 509 AD, presumably from the period of the foundation of the monastery. This monastery became the seat of the Syriac Patriarch of Antioch. The city became one of the main cities of the historical Diyaar Muḍar, the western part of the Jazira.

In the 9th century, al-Raqqah served as capital of the western half of the Abbasid Caliphate between 796 and 809 A.D. under the reign of Caliph Haroun Ar-Rashid.

During the period of the Hamadaanis (Hamdanids) in the 940s the city declined rapidly. At the end of the 10th century until the beginning of the 12th century, ar-Raqqah was controlled by Bedouin dynasties. I

In the 16th century, al-Raqqah again entered the historical record as an Ottoman customs post on the Euphrates.

The city of Al-Raqqah was resettled from 1864 onwards, first as a military outpost, then as a settlement for former Bedouin Arabs and for Chechens, who came as refugees from the Caucasian war theaters in the middle of the 19th century.

In the 1950s, the worldwide cotton boom stimulated an unrecorded growth of the city, and the re-cultivation of this part of the middle Euphrates area. Cotton is still the main agricultural product of the region.

The growth of the city meant on the other hand a removal of the archaeological remains of the city's great past. The palace area is now almost covered with settlements, as well as the former area of the ancient ar-Raqqa (today Mishlab) and the former Abbasid industrial district (today al-Mukhtalṭa). Only parts were archaeologically explored. The 12th-century citadel was removed in the 1950s (today Dawwar as-Sa'a, the clock-tower circle). In the 1980s rescue excavations in the palace area began as well as the conservation of the Abbasid city walls with the Baab Baghdad and the two main monuments within the city, the Abbasid mosque and the Qasr al-Banaat.

ISIL Rips the Syrian Arab Cultural Heritage

As the people of the Syrian Arab Republic continue to endure incalculable human suffering and loss, their country's rich tapestry of cultural heritage is being ripped to shreds. World Heritage sites have suffered considerable and sometimes irreversible damage. Four of them are being used for military purposes or have been transformed into battlefields: Palmyra; the Crac des Chevaliers; the Saint Simeon Church in the Ancient villages of Northern Syria; and Aleppo, including the Aleppo Citadel.

Archaeological sites are being systematically looted and the illicit trafficking of cultural objects has reached unprecedented levels.

There are alarming reports that Syrian heritage has been deliberately targeted for ideological reasons. Human representations in art are being destroyed by extremist and fanatics' intent on eradicating unique testimonies of Syria's rich cultural diversity.

All layers of Syrian culture were attacked --including pre-Christian, Christian and Islamic.

The destruction of such precious heritage gravely affects the identity and history of the Syrian people and all humanity, damaging the foundations of society for many years to come. The protection of cultural heritage, both tangible and intangible, is inseparable from the protection of human lives, and should be an integral part of humanitarian and peace building efforts.

ISIS Last Stand; End of the Myth of the Islamic State (Daesh) for the Caliphate

A historical note that should be remembered that there's nothing civil about United Sates of America's war on Syria, launched by the Obama administration in March 2011, orchestrated by Hillary Clinton, using ISIS and other terrorists as imperial foot soldiers, aiming for regime change, wanting the country transformed into another US vassal state.

Russia's intervention in September 2015 changed the dynamic on the ground, turning likely defeat into triumph – ISIS smashed, pockets of its fighters being mopped up, attacks on al-Nusra terrorists continuing to eliminate them as a threat.

There can be no doubt about it, the ISIS of just two years ago was the most powerful, well-led, generously-armed and resource-efficient paramilitary force in modern history, having carved out for itself an empire between two sovereign states and devastating their armies in the process. However, this is no longer so. The days of the Islamic State consuming Syria like a cancer are over.

Clearly, Russia and its allies have expelled ISIS from its last urban stronghold in Syria allowing the Syrian coalition to turn its attention to the numerous hotspots around the country where al Qaida-linked groups have dug in waiting for the Syrian Army to make its final push.

Lebanese media reported that the Syrian Arab Army (SAA), joined by combat troops from the Iranian Revolutionary Guard Corps (IRGC) and Hezbollah, recaptured the city of Abu Kamal in Deir El Zor province. The city was the last bastion for the terrorist group, ISIS, which, at one time, controlled a vast swathe of land stretching from northern Iraq to central Syria.

History will record the 20th of November 2017 as the turning point in the Middle Eastern region that terminates what was called a Caliphate or Islamic State by restoring the border city with Iraq, Al-Bu Kamal city, where the last ISIS group was eliminated in totality. The liberated city returned to its people in the Syrian Arab Republic.

The active phase of the military operation in Syria is nearly over. Thanks to the joint efforts, terrorists are being wiped out in the Al-Bu Kamal area in eastern Syria and along the Syrian-Iraqi border. It will only be a matter of time before the other militant groups are completely eradicated which will allow The Syrian Arab Republic to move on to a post-conflict settlement and stabilization.

Termination the myth "Islamic State" does not mean its Wahabis' ideology is destroyed. This ideology still causes danger as it is deeply rooted in most of those fanatic Islamist Salafist limited way of thinking which does not agree with human mind logic and free thinking.

Dr. Bashar Al-Assad Parliament Speech

In a landmark speech at the Syrian People's Assembly, the Syrian Parliament [34], President Assad called on those who carried the weapons against the Syrians to put down their weapons and join reconciliations, asserting that terrorism would but destroy the homeland. He also underscored that the Syrians have no alternative but only victory because *"blood shedding would not end but through the eliminating of terrorism from its roots."* President Assad, asserting further continued work on the political track in reply to the State and popular desire as to end blood shedding.

He pointed out that a big part of the ongoing crisis in Syria is regional and international more than domestic, calling on the new Parliament to work on needed legislations, measures and laws as to foil the economic terrorism and other forms of terrorism imposed against the Syrians.

President Al-Assad said: *"We are witnessing international conflicts that have led to regional conflicts between countries that seek preserving their sovereignty and independence and other countries that seek implementing other parties' agendas even at the expense of their own people's interests."*

President Al-Assad said that the countries supporting terrorism were aware that their main political plan after the failure of their terrorist scheme against Syria was to target the constitution and consequently create chaos. The plan was to help terrorism be completely dominant and then be described as moderate. He pointed out that in order to perpetuate their scheme, the countries supporting terrorism kept using sectarian terms to feed sedition.

He clarified that: *"The sectarian systems turn the people of a homeland to enemies; thereby colonialist countries introduce themselves as a protector to certain groups inside this homeland."* He also stressed that unity doesn't start from geography but from the unity of the citizens.

President Al-Assad noted that the USA did not commit itself to the agreed upon regarding the conditions pertaining to cessation of hostilities, turning blind eyes to Erdogan's support to terrorism, not to mention the Saudi public support for terrorism.

Al-Assad blasted the destructive role and foreign agendas of some foreign opposition groups, whose only agenda was to wake up, sleep and eat! As well as he blasted the schemes as to target the Constitution for creating a racial sectarian constitution which would transform the united Syrians into dismembered sectarian in tatters Syrians.

President Assad reiterated that the Syrians are ever to defend their sovereignty, integrity and fight terrorism and are never to be taken by some foreign-agenda agents who are a floor cloth for their masters.

The president said that principles are essential in any negotiation process because they constitute the reference for talks, adding that from the beginning of "Geneva3", *"we presented a paper of principles on which talks can be based."*

---

[34] **Al-Assad Parliament speech on July 7, 2017**

On the Turkish role, President Al-Assad said that *"Erdogan's fascist regime has been concentrating on Aleppo because it is his last hope to achieve his brotherhood project. However, Aleppo will be the grave where the dreams of this butcher will be buried."*

He added: "Syria's war on terrorism will continue not because the Syrians like wars. The war was imposed on the country and bloodshed won't stop until terrorism with all its forms is uprooted wherever it is in Syria."

The president went on to say that any political process that doesn't start, go in parallel and end with eliminating terrorism is fruitless and meaningless, repeating his call on all who carried weapon for whatever reason to join the reconciliation process in the country. He said: *"Terrorism will inevitably be defeated as long as our brave Army, friendly countries like Russia, Iran, and China are supporting the Syrian people."*

CHAPTER FIVE
CHARTING A FUTURE FOR SYRIA

The UN Security Council at its 7855ᵗʰ meeting, on 31 December 2016 adopted Resolution 2336. The Security Council recalled all its previous resolutions and Presidential Statements on the situation in the Syrian Arab Republic, in particular 2254 (2015) and 2268 (2016), and the Geneva Communique of 30 June 2012. The council reaffirmed its strong commitment to the sovereignty, independence, unity and territorial integrity of the Syrian Arab Republic, and to the purposes and principles of the Charter of the United Nations.

The Council noted the Joint Statement by the Ministers of Foreign Affairs of the Islamic Republic of Iran, the Russian Federation and the Republic of Turkey of December 20, 2016, noting with appreciation the mediation efforts undertaken by the Russian Federation and the Republic of Turkey to facilitate the establishment of a ceasefire in the Syrian Arab Republic.

The Council welcomed and supported the efforts by Russia and Turkey to end violence in Syria and jumpstart a political process, and takes note of the documents issued by Russia and Turkey in this regard (S/2016/1133); stressing the importance of the full implementation of all relevant Security Council resolutions, particularly 2254 (2015) and 2268 (2016); and looking forward to the meeting to be held in Astana, Kazakhstan, between the Government of the Syrian Arab Republic and the representatives of the opposition viewing it as an important part of the Syrian-led political process and an important step ahead of the resumption of negotiations under the auspices of the United Nations in Geneva on 8 February 2017.

The Summit: From Geneva, Astana, Sochi to Ankara

Geneva talks that restarted in early 2016 ended in deadlock. Russia, Turkey and Iran later convened in Astana in a series of talks to establish de-escalation zones in an effort to complement the Geneva processes.

In November 2017, the Russian President Vladimir Putin, the Iranian President Hassan Rouhani, and the Turkish President Recep Tayyip Erdogan met in the Black Sea resort of Sochi for the first time to chart a plan to stabilize Syria. The summit between the three powers, all deeply involved in the conflict, is designed to pave the way for a settlement likely to leave Syria's Russian- and Iranian-backed president, Bashar al-Assad, in power within a reformed Syrian constitution [35]. It follows the near-collapse of the Syrian opposition since Moscow's armed intervention in 2015 and the military defeat of Islamic State in all of the major towns and cities that were under its control.

On April 4, 2018, Putin sat down with Erdogan and Rouhani in Ankara, capital of Turkey, for the second time and agree to discuss Syria's future since attending a similar meeting in Sochi, Russia as stated before. Russia and Iran have provided crucial support to President Bashar Assad's forces, while Turkey has backed the rebels seeking to overthrow him and that his military "won't stop" trying to oust Syrian Kurdish fighters from northern Syria. But, their influence over Syria and diplomatically isolating the United States were included on the agenda.

The leaders agreed to cooperate on reconstruction and to build a hospital in Syria's Tel 'Abyad

---

[35] **Appendix A has the draft for the reformed Syrian constitution**

to treat those injured from Eastern Ghouta, the suburbs of the Syrian capital, Damascus, as a step forward. The three countries teamed up to work for a Syria settlement despite their differences, reaffirmed their commitment to Syria's territorial integrity and the continuation of local cease-fires. They called on the international community to provide more aid for war-ravaged Syria.

Iran, Turkey and Russia have agreed to work together to solve the Syrian conflict and to accelerate efforts to stabilize war-torn Syria. Vladimir Putin Russian President said that "...*everyone must join in the common work to restore the economy and infrastructure of Syria.*"

To Putin "*The militants in Syria have sustained a decisive blow and now there is a realistic chance to end the multi-year war; and the Syrian people will have to determine their own future and agree on the principles of their own statehood. It is obvious that the process of reform will not be easy and will require compromises and concessions from all participants, including of course the government of Syria.*"[36]

Putin hosted Assad in Sochi and extracted a more soothing tone than normal. He insisted that Assad was committed to a peace process as the military de-escalation zones had reduced the levels of violence and hundreds of thousands of refugees started returning home.

To Putin reconstruction of Syria is needed, "*Given the colossal scale of the destruction it would be possible to think together about the development of a comprehensive program for Syria.*"

To President Tayyip Erdogan "*Maintaining Syria's territorial integrity depends on preserving equal distance from all terrorist organizations.*"

To Iranian President Rouhani "*the grounds for a political settlement had been laid*" but he argued that "*it was unacceptable for foreign troops not invited into Syria by the government to remain in the country,*" – a reference to US troops in the north-east of the country.

The three-way summit endorsed Putin's plan for a Syrian national dialogue congress to be held in Russia to help frame the constitution for an integrated Syria, including the terms of presidential elections in which Assad would be entitled to stand.

The United States' Destabilization Strategy in Syria

On the other side, and on January 13, 2018, the US-led Coalition reported that it would train a group called the Syrian Border Security Force (BSF), and would aim to reach 30,000 fighters, half of those being composed by current SDF members.

It was reported that the United States, by January 2018, illegally was not invited and without the Syrian government permission, was looking for a 30,000-strong force to "maintain security" along Iraq, Turkey and internal borders, but there were approximately 230 individuals training in the BSF's inaugural class, with the goal of a final force size of approximately 30,000. The BSF retrained approximately 15,000 veteran SDF fighters, and recruitment and training underway to fill the other 15,000 positions.

Officially, US Secretary of State, Rex Tillerson, gave a speech[37] pointing out that the United States would stay in Syria – open-ended – in the future and until President Bashar al-Assad has left the scene. Rex Tillerson in his speech called "*the nature of the Assad regime, like that of its sponsor Iran, is malignant. It has promoted state terror. It has empowered groups that kill American soldiers, such as

---

[36] **Patrick Wintour, diplomatic editor for the Guardian, "*Putin brings Iran and Turkey together in bold Syria peace plan,*" November 22, 2017**

[37] **Rex W. Tillerson, Secretary of State, Hoover Institute at Stanford University, Stanford, CA, January 17, 2018**

al-Qaida. It has backed Hizballah and Hamas. And it has violently suppressed political opposition. And it has violently suppressed political opposition. Bashar al-Assad's grand strategy, to the extent he has one beyond his own survival, includes hosting some of the most radical terrorist elements in the region and using them to destabilize his neighbors. Assad's regime is corrupt, and his methods of governance and economic development have increasingly excluded certain ethnic and religious groups. His human rights record is notorious the world over."

Tillerson outlined a new U.S. strategy in Syria, hinging on maintaining an indefinite military presence in the country with the goal of ousting the government of Syrian President Bashar Assad. He, specifically, promised to sustain the military campaigns against ISIS and al-Qaida affiliates, to continue the U.N.-sponsored process in Geneva that aims to produce a new government for the country, to diminish Iran's influence in Syria, to help refugees and other displaced go home, and to ensure that Syria is free of weapons of mass destruction.

I wonder whether this is the best history, context and analysis of what the underlying conflicts and the reasons for all the violence in Syria are that the United States of America's top foreign policy official allow intelligent human beings question what is so terribly deficient, narrow-minded and self-serving about US academia in this field to let university students listen to the U.S. Secretary of State making illegal decisions and interfering in Syria. There is nothing to indicate that Tillerson has a grasp on how his "strategy" for Syria relates to a more comprehensive policy for the Middle East region as a whole.

Tillerson did not mention in his speech that the US has some other policies and goals for its future presence in Syria such as building permanent bases – in a kind of base race with Russia – and supporting Kurdish forces in the Syrian side of the border to Turkey. Such acts may push Turkey closer to Russia and eventually and predictably Turkey will turn its back completely on Europe and leave NATO.

The truth was not said that the US illegal presence in Syria was to build bases and be in control of its oil resources and not about regime change. Rex's speech spelled prolonged hell for fellow human beings in Syria and – open-ended – troubles for Iran and its people. He also did not mention that the US under the Trump administration has chosen to promote and support the new fundamentalist Islamist-Zionist team, Saudi-Arabia and Israel, supported by the Gulf States, to gang up against the Iran that the US and Israel see Iran as a huge threat to them.

Calling Upon the World Community to Secure Syria from Terrorists

The World community must understand that most of the Heritage sites are destroyed and mutilated by the barbaric and criminal ISIS Wahhabi Salafist ideology in the Syrian Arab Republic. I start by calling all human beings, in the name of humanity, to save Syria's rich social mosaic and cultural heritage by protecting its World Heritage Sites, in line with UN Security Council Resolution 2139, adopted on 22 January 2014.

Stabilization is needed by calling upon the world community to condemn the use of cultural sites for military purposes and call on all parties to the conflict to uphold international obligations, notably the 1954 Hague Convention for the protection of cultural property in the event of Armed Conflict and customary international humanitarian law.

The Syrian Arab Republic appealed to all countries and professional bodies involved in customs, trade and the art market, as well as individuals and tourists, to be on alert for stolen Syrian artifacts, to verify the origin of cultural property that might be illegally imported, exported and/or offered for sale, and to adhere to the UNESCO 1970 Convention on illicit trafficking of cultural property as an important part of stabilization in Syria.

UNESCO efforts are needed to save Syria's cultural heritage which is part of wider efforts to stabilize Syria. Destroying the inheritance of the past robs future generations of a powerful legacy, deepens hatred and despair and undermines all attempts to foster reconciliation. The time is needed to stop the destruction, build peace and protect the Syrian common heritage by contributing to the reconstruction of Syria.

For the help in reconstruction efforts, Syria looked primarily to Iran, Russia and China. With businesses from these three allies were among the biggest beneficiaries of the winding down of Syria's combat in most parts of the country.

The United Nations estimated that the cost of rebuilding Syria will be at least $250 billion, and after the long-running war in Syria, peace negotiations, counter-terrorism and geo-politics continue to resolve in favor of peace and stability.

Learning relevant lessons from past conflicts requires a stronger and more realistic integration of a wide range of "stabilization" capacities of the US Government and needs to include a wider field of actors. Stabilization as a high-level political strategy provides a stronger way of looking at generating peace and incorporating lessons from recent conflicts to assist efforts towards peace in Syria.

As an Arab American, I wondered why the United States started the policy of aggression to delay the stabilization of Syria?

Trump's United States decided to react by stressing their forced presence in Syria by training a force to maintain "security" along the Syrian border as the operation against ISIS and tried to create a 30,000-strong force partly composed of veteran fighters and operate under the American term "Syrian Arab Coalition."[38] The United States, after feeling their loss in Syria decoded to use the Syrian Democratic Forces to continue with the destabilization of Syria.

Who are the Syrian Democratic Forces?

The establishment of the Syrian Democratic Forces (SDF) was announced on October 11, 2015, during a press conference in Al-Hasakah city located 50 miles south of the Turkish border-city of Qamishli in Syria, SDF is a US-backed alliance of Kurdish and Arab fighters, and the Turkish-backed Free Syrian Army (FSA), a loose entity of opposition rebel groups, mostly Kurdish, founded on the 15th of October to fight ISIS!

The SDF is mostly composed of, and militarily led by, the People's Protection Units (YPG), which was formed in 2004 as the armed wing of the Kurdish leftist Democratic Union Party. It expanded rapidly in the Syrian War and came to predominate over other armed Kurdish groups.

---

[38] **The Syrian Arab Coalition is claimed by the U.S. government as an alliance of programmatically exclusively ethnic Arab militias established during the Syrian War. In this narrative, it consists of exclusively ethnic Arab component groups of the polyethnic Syrian Democratic Forces alliance. However, no reference for the "Syrian Arab Coalition" can be found outside of the communication of the U.S. administration. The term "Syrian Arab Coalition" has been described as an invention without substance, for political communication, to mitigate Turkish aversion against U.S. support for the SDF due to the latter's strong ethnic Kurdish component**

According to the U.S. Department of Defense, the Pentagon, SDF, mostly Kurdish militia made up 40% and 60% Arabs established as a democratic and federal Syria along the lines of the "Rojava region" in the north.

President Bashar al-Assad Survived and Emerged as the Most Powerful Arab Leader

United States' Government refused to recognize the legitimacy of Syria's Government even after the first internationally monitored democratic election in all of Syria's history, which was held on June 3, 2014, and which the current candidate Bashar al-Assad, whom the US alliance has been trying to overthrow, won by 89% and Bashar al-Assad was sworn in for his third seven-year term as President of Syrian Arab Republic on July 16, 2014.

On November 14, 2017, Syrian President Bashar al-Assad has given one of the most important speeches of his political career before the Arab Forum for Confronting the Zionist-US Reactionary Alliance and Supporting the Resistance of the Palestinian People, at Sham Hotel in Damascus [39]. Several national forces, parties and figures from Lebanon, Palestine, Jordan, Egypt, Iraq, Algeria, Bahrain, Yemen and Syria participated in the forum, which was held under the auspices of President Bashar al-Assad.

The forum aimed at drawing up a plan to confront the imperialist project and supporting the Palestinians' resistance against the Israeli occupation. The participants discussed over two days the Arab parties' plan to repel the so-called "*Middle East Alliance*" which the US and Israel created to include a number of Arab reactionary forces on top being by the Saudi regime.

The forum also sought to set up another media plan that covered various media fields, including social media, to raise awareness among the Arab public opinion of the reality of these projects and their catastrophic effects on the Arab nation, in addition to developing frameworks and strategies of cooperation in the field of boycotting the Zionist entity.

Delivering a speech during the meeting, President al-Assad said that dealing with issues affecting the Arab nation and pan-Arabism requires serious work to clear up some concepts that targeted the nation, including attempts to undermine the relation between Arabism and Islam, stressing that Arabism and pan-Arabism is a civilized, cultural, and human condition.

He also stressed the need to disprove claims of there being contradiction between Arabism and Islam, as well as disproving any ethnic discourse, adding that the policies of some Arab states that worked against the interests of the Arab people have also affected pan-Arabism.

President Bashar Al-Assad has stressed in his speech [40] that "*hitting national belongingness weakens our first defense line, as a society, against cultural and intellectual invasion attempts that seek turning us into helpless machines that act according to foreign-prepared plans.*"

He added: "*the war on Syria hasn't affected the Syrians' faith in the inevitability of victory against terrorism, nor has it weakened its adherence to their identity, creed, and pan-Arab affiliation.*"

President al-Assad's speech emphasized the importance of Arabism for the 21st century as the only proven school of thought and method of government that is capable of uniting peoples across

---

[39] **Syrian Arab News Agency, "*the Arab Forum on Confronting Zionist-US Reactionary forces Alliance to be Held in Damascus*", Damascus, November 12, 2017**

[40] **Posted by Alexander Valiente, "*President Assad's Speech at the Arab Forum for Confronting the Zionist-US Reactionary Alliance,*" Internationalist News, Syria November 14, 2017.**

the Arab world in a spirit that cherishes ancient traditions and allows for all varieties of modern progress.

I understand that Arab Nationalism emerged as a distinct liberation movement in the Arab world in the first half of the 20th century. The Ba'athist movement was among the first and most successful schools of thought in defining Arab Nationalism or Arabism during the decades when Arabs were fighting for their independence against the European colonialism which flowed from the Sykes-Picot Agreement of 1916.

To President al-Assad: *"Arabism is a cultural concept that involves all ethnic groups, religions and communities. It is a civilized status to which all who once existed in the region, without exceptions, contributed,"* He added that *"the Arab language and Arab nationalism unite all these ethnic groups, communities and religions and at the same time preserve the privacy of each of them"*.

President al-Assad said that there's an organic connection between Arabism and Islam, and there is certainly no contradiction between them, stressing that it is wrong to believe that one can either be an Arab or a Muslim.

"So, undermining this relation through Islamic extremism undermines Arabism. They diverted Islam and pushed it towards extremism. It separated itself from Arabism, and Islam and Arabism became weaker. Someone might ask why I'm talking about Arabism and Islam and not Arabism and Christianity. I would say that of course this is the same relationship; the relationship between nationalism and religion, but colonialism and enemies of pan-Arabism didn't work in this direction, rather they focused on Arabism and Islam," he explained.

President Bashar al-Assad injected also a calming and assuring wisdom into a debate that is often hijacked by egotists and those purposefully spreading disinformation. The Syrian President stated that there has never been any schism, conflict nor contradiction between the values of Islam and Christianity and those of Arabism. Arabism stresses the unity, shared historic and present cultural bonds between Arabic speaking peoples. As the Noble Quran is written in Arabic, this demonstrates the harmonious nature of secular Arabism with the religion of Islam. Both are strengthened when seen as unifying forces and both literally speak a common language.

President al-Assad said that Christianity's relationship with Arabism is equally strong, but that ever since the 1920s, when the British Empire funded and helped to found the regressive Muslim Brotherhood, the enemies of the Arab peoples have attempted to use Islam as a means of destroying Arab societies where its correct interpretation is one of unity, peace and wisdom.

President al-Assad explained that the enemies of Arabism seek to destroy any thought that helps to unify the Arabs in order to mold them into machines rather than free thinking men and women, in the system of US led financial globalism. A strong, unifying movement like Arabism is a demonstrative alternative to US neo-liberal/anti-cultural globalism, which is the reason that those in Washington and its de-facto satellite states are so keen on destroying Arabism and provoking sectarianism war against it.

Today, American financial globalism has taken the place of British Imperialism as the foremost existential threat to Arabism. President al-Assad explained that the enemies of Arabism seek to destroy any thought that helps to unify the Arabs in order to mold them into machines rather than free thinking men and women, in the system of US led financial globalism. A strong, unifying movement like Arabism is a demonstrative alternative to US neo-liberal/anti-cultural globalism, which is the reason that those in Washington and its de-facto satellite states are so keen on destroying Arabism and provoking sectarianism war against it.

Many commentators remark that some of the causes of the foreign led and instigated conflict in Syria include the Qatari regime's desire to build pipeline through Syrian territory, the Zionist Yinon Plan [41] to conquer and destroy large parts of the Arab world and the Wahhabi Saudi plan to effective divide and rule the rest of Syria as a regressive Takfiri fiefdom, all with assistance from the US and European aggressors.

While these are all the specific causes of the present conflict, the overarching reason is that which historically and indeed presently, has prevented these illegal moves against the sovereignty, dignity and unity of the Syrian Arab Republic. The imperialist and Zionist powers do not need to wage war against weak, sectarian and extremist Arab states because such states have already been effectively weakened into a position where national wealth and dignity is surrendered without a fight. Instead, it is states with strong Arabism identities and a sense of independence that in the eyes of the imperialist and Zionists, must be broken in order to be exploited.

President al-Assad pointed out that this is what the imperial powers did in Libya, but that the same method did not work against Syria because of the political conditions established in the Syrian Arab Republic.

It is impossible to reject imperialism if one rejects Arabism. There is no logical, practical or workable peaceful alternative to preserving freedom in the Arab world apart from Arabism. Syria's success in vanquishing her enemies has been primarily due to the strength of Arabism in creating popular unity against a multi-front onslaught.

President Bashar al-Assad remarked that some provocateurs want to take away the title "Arab" from the Syrian Arab Army (SAA). He remarked that such moves are foolish. In calling itself an Arab Army, the SAA has managed to unite all Syrians in spite of any ethnic or religious affiliation behind a common principle of sovereignty for all the peoples of Syria.

If this unifying concept was removed, the Army would merely be a mercenary force—a kind of corporate body that could not mobilize the people will of the people. If the people were not behind the Army, it would not have been able to preserve Syria as it has done, even before its non-Arab allies such as Iran and Russia helped to finish the job.

The occupier entity represents the last breath of colonial tyranny in the Arab world and one which relies on the promotion of anti-Arabism propaganda in order to cultivate power. President Al-Assad stated that Arab unity necessitates support for Palestinian liberation as anything else would be a rejection of the unity of Arabic speaking peoples throughout the region.

This explains why it is in the Zionist interest to promote sectarian groups whose goals is

---

[41] **The term Yinon Plan refers to an article published in February 1982 in the Hebrew journal *Kivunim* ("Directions") entitled *'A Strategy for Israel in the 1980s'*. It analyzes the weaknesses of Arab countries, by citing what Yinon perceives to be flaws in their national and social structures, concluding that Israel should aim to bring about the fragmentation of the Arab world into a mosaic of ethnic and confessional groupings. 'Every kind of inter-Arab confrontation,' he argued, would prove to be advantageous to Israel in the short term. Yinon saw contemporary events in Lebanon as a foreshadowing of future developments overall throughout the Arab world. The upheavals would create a precedent for guiding Israeli short-term and long-term strategies. Specifically, he asserted that the immediate aim of policy should be the dissolution of the military capabilities of Arab states east of Israel, while the primary long-term goal should work towards the formation of unique areas defined in terms of ethnonational and religious identities.**
Yinon's ideas are that Syria would implode into confessional fragments composed of Alawate, Druze and Sunni communities were the country to be occupied after an Israel invasion, and that such an event should cause reverberations throughout the Arab world, resulting in a reconfiguration of ethnic microstates guaranteed to introduce an era of peace.

to weaken pen-Arab unity and exploit local differences, rather than allowing Arabs to focus on creating a peacefully unified realm. In this sense, Palestine will also be an implicit factor in Arabism, so long as it remains occupied.

Benjamin Netanyahu Failed Miserably in His Attempts to Convince the World that Al-Assad Must Go

Over eighty countries were involved in the war that started in March 2011 to topple the Syrian President Bashar Al-Assad. Key supporters of Syria's administration include Russia and Iran, while the U.S., Turkey and Saudi Arabia all back the terrorists ISIS calling them "rebels." The war has changed dramatically over the last seven years and is rapidly merging into much more than a battle between those who are simply for and against Syria's Al-Assad.

In support to those who wanted Bashar Al-Assad to go, the biased western mass media manufactured public support for a full-scale assault on Al-Assad to benefit both the US-centralized empire which has been plotting regime change in Syria for decades and the violent Islamist extremists of ISIS who were seeking control of the region that they failed to achieve. The mass media also created the very real probability of a direct military confrontation with Syria's allies, including Russia.

It is important to mention that the United States military was deeply engaged in Syria, in part due to Israeli pressure, to depose the existing government of President Bashar Al-Assad in Syria and replace it with a composed primarily of fragmented local jurisdictions representing tribal and religious groups rather than a unified state. Israel believes that a shattered Syria would not pose any threat to its continued possession of the occupied Golan Heights and might even offer an opportunity to expand that occupation.

But, the Israeli Security Intelligence Service, another (ISIS), and the Israeli Prime Minister Benjamin Netanyahu failed miserably and tragically. Netanyahu tried hard. He fought relentlessly. He gave his best. He shouted, screamed, and yelled at politicians who did not "understand" that Assad had to go.

But Assad thrived and survived. Israeli forces made several illegal attacks in Syria. They accused Assad of using chemical weapons. They accused Assad of killing his own people and "innocent babies." They misled US politicians to say weird and mysterious things. Much of the media perpetually declared that Assad was entirely responsible for the deaths of hundreds of thousands of innocent lives in the region.

Back in 2016, Gavin Rabinowitz wrote[42] that *"Liberman himself was running around like a buffalo saying that Assad is a "butcher" who "should be removed from power."* He added that the Israeli Defense Minister Avigdor Liberman said about the Israeli governments *"haven't had a problem with the Assad regime, for 40 years not a single bullet was fired on the Golan Heights. I have set a clear policy that we do not intervene and we have not intervened. This has not changed."*

Again, Noa Landau wrote[43] in her article that *"Netanyahu seems to concede defeat when he has recently … What has troubled us is ISIS and Hezbollah and this has not changed. The heart of the matter*

---

[42] **Gavin Rabinowitz, "Liberman says Assad is a 'butcher' who must go,"** Times of Israel, December15, 2016.
[43] **Noa Landau, "Netanyahu: Israel Has No Problem With Assad, but Cease-fire Agreements Must Be Upheld,"** Haaretz, July 12, 2018.

is preserving our freedom of action against anyone who acts against us. Second, the removal of the Iranians from Syrian territory."

Israeli ambassador to the US, Michael Oren, said way back in the on September 17, 2013 that *"Israel wanted Assad gone since start of Syria civil war"*. He quoted Netanyahu saying that *"the initial message about the Syrian issue was that we always wanted Bashar Assad to go, we always preferred the bad guys who weren't backed by Iran to the bad guys who were backed by Iran."*

But what about the terrorists that the Israelis were supporting in order to get rid of Assad? Well, Oren said *"We understand that they are pretty bad guys. Still, the greatest danger to Israel is by the strategic arc that extends from Tehran, to Damascus to Beirut. And we saw the Assad regime as the keystone in that arc. That is a position we had well before the outbreak of hostilities in Syria. With the outbreak of hostilities, we continued to want Assad to go."*

That was said in 2013, but in October 2018 and after five years of the running war in Syria, the Syrian President Bashar al-Assad is in control and has sought to restore central rule in nearly all areas of the country in recent weeks, with a particular focus on reclaiming the Syrian Golan Heights that was captured by the Zionists in June 1967, it is an area of strategic and political significance to Al-Assad regime.

The Liberation of the Yarmouk Refugee Camp in Syria from ISIS

The month of June 2018 started with the Syrian Arab Army (SAA), the allied Palestinian militias, and the government of Syria a victory by liberating of the Yarmouk Refugee Camp from ISIS.

Yarmouk camp is located outside the boundaries of Damascus in Syria and used to house about 160,000 indigenous Palestinians who were uprooted from their homes in Palestine as part of the ethnic cleansing of the Palestinians strategy by the Zionist invaders. It was the largest and most prosperous settlement of Palestinians anywhere in Syria.

Based on my own experience from the old time I spent in Syria, I would like to set the record straight and reaffirm my position that Palestinians and Syrians have strong common national aspirations. The aspiration of Palestinian refugees to return to their homes in Palestine is recognized as part of the common struggle of all Syrians. And both nations seek to reclaim from the Zionist invaders all the territories in Syria and Palestine which they occupied.

It is important to note that the government of Syria treated its hundreds of thousands of Palestinian refugees better than most Arab countries and as equals to Syrian citizens themselves. Palestinians in Syria received the same levels of free health care and education as Syrians and could rise in all areas of employment as high as their abilities carried them.

There was only one formal legal distinction between Syrians and Palestinians. Palestinians were not given Syrian citizenship – to maintain their internationally-recognized right of return to their homes in Palestine – and therefore were not allowed to participate in Syrian elections.

Furthermore, most Palestinian factions chose to locate their headquarters in Damascus, and no doubt, the Assad government was a staunch supporter of the Palestinian cause.

In 2011, a group of western countries and Arab monarchies and over 80 nations, led by the USA, unleashed scores of proxy armies of terrorist mercenaries on Syria with the purpose of achieving regime change, a scheme clearly illegal under international law allowing the Zionist invaders of Palestine to participate heavily in this regime change operation, supporting terrorist mercenaries using the illegally-occupied Golan Heights as their base to fight against the Syrian government inside of Syria.

In 2012, the so-called "Free Syrian Army" (FSA) invaded and occupied Yarmouk camp. Some Palestinian factions facilitated their entry. The FSA was soon joined by al Qaeda and other militant factions.

In 2015, ISIS entered the camp and, after some devastating warfare, drove out the other terrorist factions. The terrorists evicted many Palestinians from their homes, looted and plundered everything of value, arrested anyone with known sympathies for the government and/or religious beliefs different from theirs and proceeded to torture and execute them, sexually assaulted and/or kidnapped women and girls, turned Yarmouk into a fortified camp, and collected all the foodstuffs for themselves. As in every other terrorist enclave, most of the inhabitants promptly fled to government-held areas.

The Syrian government did not directly attack Yarmouk, it patiently armed and supported the courageous fighters of the Popular Front for the Liberation of Palestine – General Command (PFLP-GC) who, for many years, led the endless struggle against the terrorists inside the camp. In other words, the Syrian government respected the neutrality requested by the Palestinian organizations.

I would like to quote [44] that *"the patience of the Syrian hosts in allowing the Palestinian refugee population to try to reconcile its differences and take the lead in expelling ISIS and al-Qaeda and their affiliates from Yarmouk since early in the conflict is especially remarkable. In the end, the SAA took over responsibility for eliminating these terrorist groups from neighboring Hajar al-Aswad, which allowed the Palestinian militias and their Syrian allies to remove the remainder from Yarmouk, the last remaining source of terror attacks on the civilian population in Damascus. We send our sincerest congratulations to all the people of Damascus and the surrounding metropolitan area for their liberation from fear of such attacks, which they endured for seven long years."*

The people in Syria who suffered for the last seven years deserve congratulations. Their suffering gave the Syrian government the impetus to achieve recently string of victories over the terrorists. Such string of victories forced many honest people of the world to open their eyes wide and realized that what has transpired in Syria was not a "popular uprising and or a revolution", but a deadly plan by the US, its western allies, the Zionists and regional clients criminally to interfere in the domestic affairs of Syria.

The liberation of Yarmouk refugee camp was a significant milestone in Syria's struggle to regain its national sovereignty and territorial integrity. It also put a satisfying end to a chapter of disunity in Palestinian and Syrian history. They show that the Palestinian and Syrian struggles are one and the same. There can be no ultimate victory for Palestine if Syria was destroyed. There can be no ultimate victory for the Syrian people without also freeing the Palestinians from the tyranny of occupation in Palestine.

---

[44] *syriasolidritymovement.org* of the Syria Solidarity Movement on May 27, 2018.

CHAPTER SIX
ON THE WAY TO RECONSTRUCTION AND STABILIZATION

While the Syrian regime's priority since 2011 has been the conduct of military operations against opposition groups, it has never lost sight of the postwar order.

After a string of military victories following direct Russian intervention in late 2015, the regime of President Bashar al-Assad has felt more confident that it will remain in power. This has allowed it to focus on development, aid, and reconstruction—matters central to future political and economic arrangements in Syria.

Furthermore, according to the Syrian government, the reconstruction money can be found from wealthy Syrians, the BRICS group of emerging economies, and multilateral lenders not controlled by the West.

Likewise, President Bashar al-Assad insisted that the *"priority of investments in Syria will be given to the businessmen from the friendly and brotherly countries which stood by Syria in its war against terrorism."* He added: *"We won't let enemies, adversaries, and terrorists, through any means, accomplish through politics what they failed to accomplish on the battlefield and through terrorism."*

Reconstruction activities started on November 25, 2014 and for three days, the Syrian Public Works Ministry and the Syrian Commerce Chambers Federation has held the first expo for reconstruction of Syria under the titles *"The Syrians Build Syria"*, and was organized by the Syrian International Marketing Agency (SIMA), was opened at Dama Rose Hotel, with the participation of 40 local companies.

The Syrian Arab News Agency reported that the Public Works Minister Hussein Arnous told journalists that the expo, which was organized in cooperation with the Ministry, sought to bring together the companies that could take part in the reconstruction stage, asserting that there were local skills, expertise, and capitals that could carry out reconstruction with the help of companies from friendly countries.

The three-day expo features companies specializing in the fields of building and construction, real-estate, architecture, energy, technical consultations, infrastructure, mechanics, banking, transport, and insurance, in addition to showcasing equipment and technology related to reconstruction. A number of workshops and lectures supervised by the Public Works Ministry was also hold on the sideline of the expo.

Furthermore, at Al Hussein Youth City in Amman between July 15 and 18, 2017, Jordan hosted an international conference and exhibition on the future reconstruction of Syria as a chance for Jordanian companies to *"transform the Syrian crisis into a real economic opportunity and to elevate the economic burdens of hosting refugees."* Jordan's neutral position towards the Syrian crisis, its hosting of Syrian refugees and its geographic location had entitled it to host this international event to witness the participation of local, regional and international companies; and to encourage the creation of economic partnerships between companies to compete internationally for the rebuilding process of Syria.

The conference included workshops discussed challenges facing the reconstruction process, in addition to new insights into the business and opportunities in today's construction industry. Discussions also covered means of funding the rebuilding process, as well as its management and implementation in light of policies of donor countries. Over 100 exhibitors participated showing their latest innovations, discussed issues of the industry and examined opportunities for partnerships. The exhibition attracted over 25,000 visitors

The Damascus International Fair

Talking about the Damascus International Fair has many memories, I was one of over one million visitors who went to Damascus, Syria to visit the first Damascus International fair that took place during the month of September 1954. Twenty-six countries participated in the Fair, in addition to a various number of Syrian Industrial and commercial Enterprises. It covered a display area of 250,000 sqm that grew with the passage of years, and with the great crowding inside Damascus city, a new Fairground was found with wide spaces to fit the increasing of the participating countries and exhibitors, in addition to the international and Syrian companies, as well as the great number of visitors.

Damascus International Fair is the oldest Fair in the Middle East, distinguishes by its long history of activities that consider a reference for Time and Place memory.

In preparation for the return of the Fair, a new Fairground is established as one of the biggest worldwide spreading over 1.2 million sqm. It is located on the Highway between Damascus and the International Airport. The new fairground enjoys exhibition halls, services and facilities according to the most modern global standards and is one of the biggest fairgrounds worldwide.

The Fairgrounds has five external gates for cars, and ten internal gates for visitors. The new Fairgrounds could embrace several exhibitions at the same time, and it has hosted tens of specialized exhibitions, in addition to Damascus International Fair, as well as many investments.

The Damascus International Fair is an annual commercial exhibition event to be called "the Syrian economy's window to the world." [45] the Fair, since its inception in 1954 until its latest edition held in 2011, is considered a reference for time and place memory in the Middle East region and for social and popular memory on the local level, in addition to being an artistic and cultural event that many Syrian and Arab writers and intellectuals await every year.

However, after the successes and benefits it achieved, it was decided that the Fair should be held periodically by Law no. 40 for 1955, which stipulated for establishing the Directorate of the Damascus International Fair and its lottery event.

I remember that in 1958, Damascus International Fair became a member of the International Fairs Union and in 1970 it achieved a qualitative leap in terms of the increased number of the participating companies and countries that covered the five continents.

This famous and well-reputed Fair has defied all the extremely harsh coercive economic measures imposed unilaterally on Syria to be revived as the 59th year fair that was hold on August 17-26, 2017 surpassing all the repercussions of the war and succeeding to attract many Arab and foreign companies to join its activities.

On August 17, 2017 Syrian officials oversaw the opening of the first Damascus International Exhibition since the start of the Syrian uprising. Reflecting the victory on display in Damascus, the exhibition—an international trade fair—has been heavily promoted by the Assad regime, presented as a symbol of its victory over the insurgency that began in 2011.

After a six-year cancellation because of the global war launched against Syria since 2011, the

---

[45] **Syrian Arab News Agency (SANA) "Damascus International Fair to be held against all odds" 24 May 2017**

Damascus International Fair reopened, launching its 59th session. Forty-five countries have raised their flags in Damascus and joined this historic city in celebration. The 60th Damascus International Fair took place from 5 to 15 September, 2018 with 46 countries challenging the war and the sanctions, joined the Damascus international fair.

Concisely, Damascus International Fair, the Syrian economy's window to the world, is brought back to life again after several years of forced absence due to the terrorist war inflicted upon the country.

This occasion has the value of being an economic, cultural, social and artistic demonstration. Only those countries and companies that had proved loyal to the Syrian government were invited, and together they discussed the future reconstruction of Syria.

The big winners of the fair were China, Russia and Iran whose companies took center stage at the fair and will soon take a primary role in rebuilding the parts of Syria that have been damaged by years of war and foreign funded chaos.

For ordinary Syrians who attended, the fair was a symbol that their country is slowly returning to normalcy and that the secular government which provides for equal rights between religious and ethnic sects as well as equality between men and women is more determined than ever to build a modern country that reflects the real values of the determined Syrian people. I consider this event to be the start of the reconstruction and rebuilding of Syria.

The devastation suffered by Syria is immense and virtually unquantifiable. Even by the most conservative estimates, the war's death toll is in the hundreds of thousands, with a similar number maimed and incapacitated. The destruction of infrastructure and all signs of civilized life, while clearly uneven, condemns large stretches of Syria to a long period of pre-modern existence. With nearly half of the population displaced, the social fabric of this once proud nation is deeply damaged. The current drive for the reconstruction of Syria—spearheaded by the Damascus regime and its backers in Russia and Iran—is a legitimate effort of rebuilding and relief and to rebuild what the war has destroyed.

The desire to rebuild Syria is sincere, many external actors ought to be held responsible in the Syrian tragedy—either for their actions or a failure to act. But, backed by Russia and Iran, Assad regime declared victory and demanded Syria's reinstatement in the international community as the legitimate government of Syria. The call for international participation in the reconstruction of Syria is part of these efforts to normalize the regime.

The Assad regime in Syria is indeed entitled to its victory: it has regained control of much of the Syrian territory, and is set to launch an offensive that would complete its control over all the Syrian territories. Reconstruction of Syria will grow continuously to restore Syria and its population to prosperity that it used to enjoy.

Geneva Conferences on Syria

The first Geneva Conference on Syria was held on June 30th 2012, in Geneva, Switzerland, initiated by the then United Nations peace envoy to Syria Kofi Annan and attended by US Secretary of State Hillary Clinton, Russian Foreign Minister Lavrov, a representative of China, British Foreign Secretary Hague, and Kofi Annan. The conference agreed on the need for a "*transitional government body with full executive powers*" which could include members of the present Syrian government and of the opposition[46]. On January 22nd 2014, *Geneva II Conference* aimed at bringing Syrian government and opposition together to discuss a transitional government, but no agreement was reached,

On January 29th 2016, *Geneva III Conference*, at the first day, Syrian government and opposition refused to sit in the same room together. On February 3 2016, UN envoy Staffan de Mistura suspended the peace talks.[47]

The Geneva peace talks on Syria in 2017, also called the *Geneva IV, V, VI, VII and VIII talks*, were peace negotiations between the Syrian government and the Syrian opposition under the auspices of the United Nations. ... The *Geneva VII talks* began on July 10, 2017

Geneva IV Conference, under the auspices of the United Nations, began on February 23rd 2017 and concluded on March 3rd. The government delegation sought to focus on counter-terrorism while the opposition sought to focus on political transition.[48]

In the fifth round, or *Geneva V Conference,* United Nations-brokered Syrian peace talks ended about how they started: without a major breakthrough expected to near ending the six-year-long civil war, and the chief mediator passing the buck to continue to another round of talks.[49]

UN Special Envoy for Syria Staffan de Mistura says the Syrian government delegation refused to engage at the Geneva peace talks. UN-sponsored talks in Geneva designed to end the Syrian civil war have collapsed, with a deflated special envoy Staffan de Mistura admitting *"a golden big opportunity"* had been missed. He largely blamed the Syria government delegation for setting preconditions on holding direct talks with the opposition, saying it would be difficult for any future talks sponsor to make progress "if the government is not willing to meet anyone who has a different opinion."[50]

In short, the Syrian government delegation had refused to discuss two of the major potential agenda items – a constitutional process and presidential elections – insisting instead it would only discuss terrorism. The end of talks left the Geneva process in its eighth round of talks without credibility.

The Astana Peace Process Continues…:

The Astana Peace Process started in Kazakhstan which offered *"a platform for the talks and will not be taking part in the negotiations."* Astana was chosen as a suitable platform to host these negotiations due to the fact that Kazakhstan is objective and neutral in its approach, as well as a reliable partner for all nations. The Astana process is expected to offer a chance for the speediest settlement of the Syrian conflict through political means.

---

[46] **BBC, *"UN envoy calls for transitional government in Syria"*, June 30th 2012**
[47] **BBC, *"Syria conflict: sides trade blame over talks' suspension"*, February 4th 2016.**
[48] **Reuters, *"Russia and Syria say opposition trying to wreck peace talks"*, March 2nd 2017**
[49] **Kurdish media network (Rudaw), *"Geneva V ends with UN mediator pleading for ceasefire in Syria"*, March 31, 2017**
[50] **Patrick Wintour, *"Golden opportunity' lost as Syrian peace talks collapse"*, The Guardian, December 14th 2017**

The first Meeting

The *first meeting* was arranged with the intention of strengthening the ceasefire signed on December 30, 2016. These were indirect talks between Syrian armed rebel factions and representatives of the Syrian government, supported by Russia, Iran and Turkey, with UN delegation acting as intermediary, as well as US delegation as an observer.

These talks are credited as being the first to include both the Syrian government and an armed opposition. Its outcome was the agreement to establish a tripartite mechanism to monitor the ceasefire in Syria; expressed their readiness to cooperate in combating ISIS and An-Nusra; agreed to hold meetings on the Astana platform on specific issues. The talks took place on 23 and 24 January 2017. The first day ended without the sides reaching an agreement. The Astana Process talks aimed to support the framework in accordance with the UN Security Council Resolution 2254 and ended on the 24th with an agreement between Iran, Russia, and Turkey to form a joint monitoring body to work to enforce the Resolution 2254 ceasefire.

The Joint statement reaffirmed their commitment to the sovereignty, independence, unity and territorial integrity of the Syrian Arab Republic as a multi-ethnic, multi-religious, non-sectarian and democratic State, as confirmed by the UN Security Council.

Iran, Russia, Turkey expressed their conviction that there is no military solution to the Syrian conflict and that it can only be solved through a political process based on the implementation of the UN Security Council resolution 2254 in its entirety; and reiterate their determination to fight jointly against ISIL/DAESH and Al-Nusra and to separate from them armed opposition groups.

They supported the willingness of the armed opposition groups to participate in the next round of negotiations to be held between the government and the opposition under the UN auspices in Geneva as of February 8, 2017.

The Second Meeting

Followed by *the second meeting* in *February 15-16, 2017* for the three guarantor countries (Russia, Iran and Turkey) as well as representatives from the Syrian government and armed Syrian opposition groups, with the United Nations, the US and Jordan as observers and agreed to establish a Joint Monitoring Group, the results of which would be reported to the UN; agreed on a draft provision on reconciled areas in Syria; discussed a draft provision on the exchange of prisoners

The third Meeting

The *third meeting* took place in *March 14-15, 2017*, and was attended by representatives of Russia, Turkey and Iran, as well as the Syrian government delegation. Delegations of the UN, the US and Jordan participated as observers to review the current state of ceasefire in Syria and the situation in reconciled areas.

The Joint Statement emphasizes the firm resolve of Russia, Iran and Turkey to help strengthen the sovereignty, independence and territorial integrity of the Syrian Arab Republic. The guarantor states reviewed the current state of ceasefire in Syria and the situation in reconciled areas; discussed a provision on the working group on the exchange of detained and imprisoned persons as well as prospects for establishing a working group on Syrian Constitution and creating a single map indicating positions of terrorist groups such as ISIS and Jabhat an-Nusra and locations of the armed opposition groups. They also addressed the issue of demining the UNESCO World Heritage sites in Syria.

The Fourth Meeting

The *fourth meeting* of the Astana talks took place on the 3rd and 4th of May 2017 included delegations from the guarantor states: Russia, Iran and Turkey, and representatives of the Syrian government and Syrian armed opposition. A delegation from the United States, United Nations and Jordan all participated as observers.

The guarantor states signed a Memorandum on the *creation of de-escalation zones* in Syria. According to the Memorandum, the de-escalation areas in Idlib, Homs, Eastern Ghouta, as well as Deraa and Al-Quneitra would be created with the aim to put a prompt end to violence, improve the humanitarian situation and create favorable conditions to advance political settlement of the conflict in the Syrian Arab Republic. They adopted a Joint Statement, reaffirming their commitment to the sovereignty, independence, unity and territorial integrity of Syria. They also expressed their conviction that the solution of the Syrian conflict is possible only through political means.

The Fifth Meeting

The *Fifth International high-level meeting* within the framework of the Astana Process on Syria was held in Astana on *July 4-5, 2017*. Delegations of the ceasefire regime's guarantor states – Russia, Turkey, and Iran, as well as the government of the Syrian Arab Republic and the Syrian armed opposition, the Special Representative of the UN Secretary General for Syria Staffan de Mistura took part in the negotiations, with the representatives of Jordan and the United States participating as observers.

The outcomes of the two-day meeting were announced during a plenary session where all the parties were present. The document states *"a significant reduction in the level of violence on the ground in Syria following the signing on May 4, 2017, of the Memorandum on the creation of de-escalation areas in the Syrian Arab Republic"*. The guarantor states welcomed the establishment of the Joint Working Group on de-escalation in accordance with the Memorandum and approved its provision. The document stresses the progress in determining the boundaries of de-escalation zones. It also sets the task of finalizing the operational and technical conditions for the areas' operation.

In short, this meeting did not produce any result as parties still had some technical differences with regard to the practical implementation of the de-escalation zones plan.

The Joint Working Group scheduled the sixth meeting to take place in Iran on *August 1-2, 2017* but was postponed to mid-September as all reports that came from the Russia's foreign ministry and its partners said that Russia, Turkey and Iran were working on setting up the final de-escalation zone in Syrian Idlib province.

But regardless of every good thing Astana format has already produced, postponing the next round of talks was just another confirmation that the parties still did not reach a consensus and had nothing to come with. In the end, it added nothing to the Astana format effectiveness.

Therefore, the talks in Astana complemented the Geneva talks, implying a shift towards the Syrian opposition conducting military operations and away from Syrians with only political influence.

The Sixth Meeting

The *sixth meeting* took place on *September 14-15, 2017* focused on the details of the fourth de-escalation zone, in Syria's western Idlib Province, where significant concentrations of Takfiri terrorists, most notably from al-Nusra Front, are operating. The Russian delegation to the talks was led by Russian president's Syrian settlement envoy Alexander Lavrentyev. The Iranian delegation was led by Deputy Foreign Minister Hossein Ansari, and the Turkish delegation was led by Deputy Foreign Minister Sedat Onal. The UN Secretary General's special envoy for Syria, Staffan de Mistura, the Jordanian Foreign Ministry's special advisor for political issues Nawaf Uasfi Tel, and US Acting Assistant Secretary of State for the Near East Affairs, David Satterfield acted as observers at the consultations. Bashar Ja'afari, the Syrian ambassador to the United Nations headed the Syrian government delegation and the chief of staff of the Syrian Free Army, Ahmed Berri represented the armed opposition.

The declaration of the Idlib de-escalation area constituted the final stage in the implementation of the memorandum signed with a view to de-escalating the tension on the ground in Syria that decreased the number of ceasefire violations.

During the sixth round of talks, it was emphasized that the parties would continue their task of combatting terrorist organizations associated with DAESH and al-Qaeda. Another crucial decision to establish a *"Turkish-Russian-Iran Coordination Center"* to organize the activities in the de-escalation zones.

The Seventh Meeting

The *seventh round* of the Astana meetings was held on *October 30-31, 2017* with the participation of representatives from the three guarantor states including Iran, Russia, and Turkey, as well as the Damascus government and opposition, the United Nations, Jordan and the United States. The negotiations failed to reach an agreement on the two key points regarding the demining and exchange of detainees, the three guarantor states released a joint statement at the conclusion of the two-day meeting which included agreements on implementation of the de-escalation deal, advancing the political process, further increase of international humanitarian aid, and convening a congress to bring about a lasting political solution to the ongoing conflict in the country. The outcome of this summit disapproved the formation of a terror corridor in Northern Syria and Iraq.

The Eighth Meeting

The ministerial meeting on Syria in Astana that took place on March 16, 2018 extended the ceasefire in the De-escalation zones and gave Russia, Iran and Turkey an opportunity to compare notes. In a little more than a year, Astana has held eight rounds of Syrian talks attended by the parties to the conflict. The Astana process brought a reign of peace, presented the opportunity for the Syrian government to redesign and restructure the conflict in its favor; and enabling it to intensify its struggle against the Islamic State (IS) in Eastern Syria without worrying about the activities of the opposition in the West.

The Ninth Meeting

The ninth Astana Process talks on Syria ended May 15, 2018 in the Kazakh capital. The three guarantor states reaffirmed their commitment to maintaining a ceasefire regime and four de-escalation zones established in the war-torn country based on the agreement the three states signed in May 2017. A joint resolution issued by the three states said the next meeting will be in Sochi in July 2017.

In their resolution, Iran, Russia and Turkey emphasized the need to create conditions for the Syrian people to *"restore normal and peaceful life and to this end ensure rapid, safe and unhindered humanitarian access and safe and voluntary return of refugees and internally displaced persons to their original places of residence as well as free movement of local population."*

The guarantor states emphasized commitment to Syria's sovereignty, independence and territorial integrity and continuing the war against terrorist organizations until defeating them.

The Tenth Meeting

The tenth round of Astana format meeting kicked off in the Russian city of Sochi with the participation of the Syrian Arab Republic delegation headed by Dr. Bashar al-Jaafari and the other delegations on the 25th of June 2018.

SANA's delegate to Sochi said that a number of meetings are scheduled to be held between delegations of the guarantor states of Astana process namely (Russia, Iran and Turkey) and the participating delegations.

The delegate noted that the Russian delegation, headed by Russian President's Special Envoy for Syria, Alexander Lavrentiev, held a meeting with UN Special Envoy for Syria Staffan de Mistura

In addition to the delegations of the three guarantor states of Astana process, a UN delegation and a delegation of the "opposition" will participate in the meeting.

The US did not send representatives to Sochi as a desire to lower the importance of the Astana format and discredit the implementation of the mediatory efforts in Syrian affairs that Washington is unable to put under its control. Moreover, the United States' call to prioritize the Geneva format, including under the pretext of aiding the UN Secretary-General's Special Envoy for Syria Staffan de Mistura, looks disingenuous, given the UN envoy's concerned personal involvement in the Sochi event.

The Eleventh Meeting

The *Eleventh meeting* of Syria peace talks in Astana started in the Kazakh capital on July 4th 2018, after a six-month recess, the guarantor countries of Turkey, Russia, and Iran met once again in Astana to exchange views on various topics.

The ceasefire in Syria's northwestern province of Idleb, efforts to establish a constitutional committee that will rewrite the country's constitution and the release of prisoners are expected to top the agenda.

The meeting is attended by the guarantor countries and the Bashar al-Assad regime, and the Syrian military opposition. The United Nations and Jordan attended the meeting as observers. The US had not sent an official to the last two meetings.

On July 5th, 2018, the Syrian Negotiation Commission submitted a list of 50 candidates to represent the Syrian opposition in the constitutional committee to UN's outgoing Syria envoy Staffan de Mistura.

Under the terms of the deal, opposition groups in Idleb remained in areas in which they are already present, while Russia and Turkey carried out joint patrols in the area to prevent a resumption of fighting.

Despite the ceasefire agreement, the Assad regime and its allies continue their low-intensity attacks on Idleb's de-escalation zone.

The Twelfth Meeting

The Islamic Republic of Iran, the Russian Federation and the Republic of Turkey as guarantors of the Astana format met on the 28th and 29th November 2018 and came out with the following joint statement:

1. Reaffirmed their strong commitment to the sovereignty, independence, unity and territorial integrity of the Syrian Arab Republic and to the purposes and principles of the UN Charter;
2. Highlighted that these principles should be universally respected and that any action that might violate them and undermine achievements of the Astana format should be avoided;
3. Rejected all attempts to create new realities on the ground under the pretext of combating terrorism and expressed their determination to stand against separatist agendas aimed at undermining the sovereignty and territorial integrity of Syria as well as the national security of neighboring countries;
4. Discussed the current situation on the ground in Syria, took stock of the recent developments following their last meeting in Sochi on 30-31 July 2018 and underscored their determination to strengthen their trilateral coordination in light of their agreements;
5. Examined in details the situation in the Idlib de-escalation area and reaffirmed their determination to fully implement the Memorandum on Stabilization of the Situation in the Idlib De-escalation Area of 17 September 2018. In this regard they expressed their concern with the ongoing violations of the ceasefire regime, and declared that, as guarantors of the ceasefire regime, they would step up their efforts to ensure observance with it, including by enhancing work of the Joint Iranian-Russian-Turkish Coordination Center. They stressed the importance of a lasting ceasefire while underlining the necessity to continue effective fight against terrorism. They also emphasized that under no circumstances the creation of the above-mentioned de-escalation area should undermine the sovereignty, independence, unity and territorial integrity of the Syrian Arab Republic;
6. Reaffirmed their determination to continue cooperation in order to ultimately eliminate DAESH/ISIL, Nusra Front and all other individuals, groups, undertakings and entities associated with Al-Qaeda or DAESH/ISIL as designated by the UN Security Council. They

called upon all armed opposition groups in Syria to completely and immediately dissociate from the above-mentioned terrorist groups;

7. Strongly condemned any use of chemical weapons in Syria and demanded that any reports in this regard should be investigated promptly and professionally in full compliance with the Convention on the Prohibition of the Development, Production, Stockpiling and Use of Chemical Weapons and on Their Destruction and by the OPCW as the main international competent authority to establish use of chemical weapons;

8. Underlined their firm conviction that there could be no military solution to the Syrian conflict and that the conflict could be resolved only through the Syrian-led and Syrian-owned, UN-facilitated political process in line with the UN Security Council resolution 2254;

9. Reaffirmed their determination to step up joint efforts to launch the Constitutional Committee in Geneva, that would enjoy support of the Syrian parties, in accordance with the decisions of the Syrian National Dialogue Congress in Sochi and decided to intensify their consultations on all the levels to finalize its establishment at the soonest possible time;

10. Welcomed the successful development of the "pilot project" within the framework of the Working Group on the release of detainees/abductees and handover of the bodies as well as the identification of missing persons. The release of the detainees on 24 November 2018 constituted a step forward in implementing confidence-building measures between Syrian parties to contribute to the viability of the political process and normalization of the situation on the ground. In this regard they reiterated their commitment to further advance the efforts of the Working group;

11. Emphasized the need to continue all efforts to help all Syrians restore normal and peaceful life as well as alleviate their sufferings. In this regard, they called upon the international community, particularly the United Nations and its humanitarian agencies, to increase their assistance to Syria by providing additional humanitarian aid, restoring humanitarian infrastructure assets, including water and power supply facilities, schools and hospitals;

12. Highlighted the need to create conditions for the safe and voluntary return of refugees and internally displaced persons (IDPs) to their original places of residence in Syria. They reaffirmed their readiness to continue interaction with all relevant parties, including the Office of the United Nations High Commissioner for Refugees (UNHCR) and other specialized international agencies, in particular in the context of rendering assistance to preparing and convening the International conference on Syrian refugees and internally displaced persons (IDPs);

13. Expressed their appreciation to Mr.Staffan de Mistura, the UN Secretary-General Special Envoy on Syria, for his efforts to seek peaceful solution for the Syrian crisis and for his constructive interaction and cooperation with the Astana format during his mission;

14. Expressed their sincere gratitude to the President of the Republic of Kazakhstan, His Excellency Nursultan Nazarbayev and the Kazakh authorities for hosting in Astana the 11th International Meeting on Syria;

15. Decided to hold the next International Meeting on Syria in Astana in early February 2019.

The Thirteenth Meeting

While on August 1-2, 2019, the Kazakh capital hosted *the 13th round* of the International Meeting on Syria. The joint statement as a result of the meeting, the guarantor states of the Astana process (Russia, Iran and Turkey) states that they:

1. Reaffirmed their strong commitment to the sovereignty, independence, unity and territorial integrity of the Syrian Arab Republic and to the purposes and principles of the UN Charter;
2. Reaffirmed in this regard the respect for universally recognized international legal decisions, including those provisions of the relevant UN resolutions rejecting the occupation of Syrian Golan, first and foremost UN Security Council resolution 497;
3. Reviewed in detail the situation in the Idlib de-escalation area and highlighted the necessity to establish calm on the ground by fully implementing all agreements on Idlib, first and foremost the Memorandum of 17 September 2018. They expressed serious concern with the increased presence of the terrorist organization «Hayat Tahrir al-Sham» in the area and reaffirmed the determination to continue cooperation in order to ultimately eliminate DAESH/ISIL, Al-Nusra Front and all other individuals, groups, undertakings and entities associated with Al-Qaeda or DAESH/ISIL, and other terrorist groups, as designated by the UN Security Council. While deploring civilian casualties, they agreed to undertake concrete measures, based on the previous agreements, to ensure the protection of the civilian population in accordance with the international humanitarian law as well as the safety and security of the military personnel of the guarantors present within and outside the Idlib de-escalation area;
4. Discussed the situation in the north-east of Syria and emphasized that long-term security and stability in this region can only be achieved on the basis of respect for the sovereignty and territorial integrity of the country;
5. Rejected in this regard all attempts to create new realities on the ground under the pretext of combating terrorism, including illegitimate self-rule initiatives, and expressed their determination to stand against separatist agendas aimed at undermining the sovereignty and territorial integrity of Syria as well as threatening the national security of neighboring countries;
6. Expressed their conviction that there could be no military solution to the Syrian conflict and reaffirmed their commitment to advance the Syrian-led and Syrian owned, UN-facilitated political process in line with the UN Security Council resolution 2254 and the decisions of the Syrian National Dialogue Congress in Sochi;
7. Held detailed consultations on the trilateral basis as well as with the representatives of the Office of the United Nations Secretary-General's Special Envoy for Syria Geir O. Pedersen on the conclusion of formation and launching of the Constitutional Committee in Geneva, in accordance with the decisions of the Syrian National Dialogue Congress in Sochi. They expressed satisfaction with the progress made on finalization of the composition and the rules of procedure of the body and reiterated their readiness to facilitate the convening of the committee as soon as possible;
8. Welcomed the fourth successful operation on mutual release of detainees/abductees held on 31 July 2019 within the framework of the respective Working Group of the Astana format. They underscored that the Working Group was a unique mechanism, that had proved to

be effective and necessary for building confidence between the Syrian parties, and agreed to take measures to continue and step up its work;

9. Emphasized the need to increase humanitarian assistance to all Syrians throughout the country without preconditions. In order to support the improvement of the humanitarian situation in Syria and the progress in the process of the political settlement, they called upon the international community, the United Nations and its humanitarian agencies, to enhance the assistance to Syria, inter alia by developing early recovery projects, including the restoration of basic infrastructure assets - water and power supply facilities, schools and hospitals as well as the humanitarian mine action. They also discussed the idea and exchanged views on the perspectives of holding the International Conference on the Humanitarian Assistance to Syria;

10. Highlighted the need to facilitate safe and voluntary return of refugees and internally displaced persons (IDPs) to their original places of residence in Syria, ensuring their right to return and right to be supported. In this regard they called upon the international community to provide appropriate contributions and reaffirmed their readiness to continue interaction with all relevant parties, including the Office of the United Nations High Commissioner for Refugees (UNHCR) and other specialized international agencies;

11. Welcomed the participation of the delegations of Iraq and Lebanon as new observers of the Astana format. They expressed their conviction that the observers (Iraq, Jordan and Lebanon) would contribute to the efforts to bring peace and stability in Syria;

12. Expressed their sincere gratitude to the Kazakh authorities for hosting in Nur-Sultan the 13th International Meeting on Syria in the Astana format;

13. Decided to hold the next International Meeting on Syria in the Astana format in Nur-Sultan in October 2019.

The Second Brussels' Conference on the Syrian Conflict and Its Impact on the Region.

On 24 April, 2018, the European Union (EU) and the United Nations co-chaired the second Brussels Conference on Supporting the future of Syria and the region, the EU organized a "day of dialogue" with Non-Governmental Organizations (NGOs) from Syria and the region. More than 200 NGOs met in Brussels to offer operational recommendations to the ministerial part of the conference the following day. A session with the representatives of the Syrian civil society was also organized in the run-up to the Conference. Representatives from both the NGOs and civil society intervened during the plenary sessions on 25 April, enabling the voice of Syrians to be heard directly by the international community as it considered how to support the future of the country and of the region. [51]

The conference succeeded in mobilizing aid to Syrians inside the country and in the neighboring countries, including for hosting communities, through pledges totaling $ 4.4 billion for 2018, as well as multi-year pledges of $ 3.4 billion for 2019-2020.

The conference was the opportunity to gather political support for the UN-led peace process.

---

[51] **http://www.consilium.europa.eu/en/meetings/international-ministerial-meetings/2018 /04/24-25/. "Supporting the future of Syria and the region – Brussels conference, 24-25/04/2018," European Council, Council of the European Union, conference agenda,**

Federica Mogherini, High Representative for Foreign Affairs and Security Policy said: "*There was common ground in reconfirming that there is no military solution to the war in Syria. There is a need, recognized by everybody, to relaunch the political process. There is also agreement on the key role of the UN in leading this process. This is extremely important because the EU has always regarded the UN - and Staffan de Mistura - as the only ones having legitimate leadership to ensure that the political process is meaningful, inclusive, and represents all Syrians in intra-Syrian talks, and that this takes place in line with the UNSC resolutions already adopted.*"

While *Mark Lowcock, UN Under-Secretary-General for Humanitarian Affairs and Emergency Relief Coordinator said: "It is important that we continue to deliver results to the people of Syria through the finance we raise. One of my top messages to those financing us is that the money you provide makes a difference to the lives of Syrians caught up in this horrible crisis. There is absolutely no question that without conferences of this sort, and without the financing we secure, things would be a lot worse.*"

On May 4, 2017, the High Representative of the European Union for Foreign Affairs and Security Policy and Vice-President of the European Commission, the Emergency Relief Coordinator and Under-Secretary-General for Humanitarian Affairs of the United Nations and the Foreign Ministers of Germany, Kuwait, Norway, Qatar, and the United Kingdom chaired in Brussels a conference on the Syrian conflict and its impact on the region. [52]

This conference brought together representatives of over 70 countries and international organizations, international and Syrian civil society, and built on previous years' conferences in Kuwait and London.

The conference stressed the importance of maintaining a sovereign, independent, unitary and territorially integral country where all Syrians will be able to live in peace and security and recognized that the humanitarian and resilience needs of vulnerable people (especially women and children) inside Syria and in the region have never been greater. It took note of UN-coordinated appeals requesting $8 billion in 2017 to cover assistance and protection needs inside Syria as well as in Turkey, Lebanon, Jordan, Iraq and Egypt.

Participants re-iterated their full support and commitment to the UN-moderated intra-Syrian talks in Geneva, as the only forum where a political solution should be negotiated and recognized the constructive role that regional actors can play in facilitating a resolution to the conflict and welcomed the initiative of the EU to find common ground between them on the future of Syria. They also considered that the Astana meetings have a potentially crucial role in consolidating and strengthening the nationwide ceasefire, guaranteed by Russia and Turkey, and, now, with the participation of Iran. Constructive contributions from the Astana meetings should complement the efforts of the Geneva Task Forces.

Participants condemned the continued violations and abuses of international humanitarian law (IHL) and international human rights law by parties involved in the conflict, including the deliberate targeting of civilians and civilian infrastructure, in particular medical and educational infrastructure and places of worship. They condemned the atrocities committed by ISIL/Daesh and other UN-designated terrorist groups and reaffirmed their strong commitment to defeat them.

Participants acknowledged that reconstruction will be successful only in the context of a genuine and inclusive transition that benefits all the Syrians and that Reconstruction and international support for its implementation will be a peace dividend only once a credible political transition is firmly underway.

---

[52] **Foreign affairs and international relations, *European Council: "Supporting the future of Syria and the region: co-chairs declaration"* May, 2017**

The conference has agreed on a comprehensive approach to the Syrian crisis. It underlined the need to continue to respond to the dire humanitarian situation by ensuring principled assistance and protection for those populations in need and support to the neighboring countries. The scale of suffering is such that a political solution is more urgent than ever before. Investment of political efforts in supporting a resolution to the crisis is therefore paramount in securing a future for Syria and its people. Only Syrians can make the agreement that will secure peace. But the commitment of the international community and the region to supporting them in achieving that peaceful future is essential. Sustainable and inclusive peace in Syria for the Syrians remains the objective of all our efforts.

The Commitment of the 10th BRICS Summit Meeting[53] toward Syria

The Summit group reaffirmed their commitment for a political resolution of the conflict in Syria, through an inclusive "Syrian-led, Syrian-owned" political process that safeguards the state sovereignty, independence and territorial integrity of Syria, in pursuance of United Nations Security Council Resolution 2254 of the year 2015 and taking into account the result of the Congress of the Syrian National Dialogue in Sochi and reaffirmed their commitment to a peaceful resolution in Syria and their opposition to measures that run contrary to the UN Charter and the authority of the United Nations Security Council (UNSC) and that do not contribute to advancing the political process. They also highlighted the importance of unity in the fight against terrorist organizations in Syria in full observance of the relevant UNSC Resolutions. They called for enhanced efforts to provide necessary humanitarian assistance to the Syrian people, bearing in mind urgent reconstruction needs.

Idlib

Idlib is the last unconquered de-escalation zone of the four that were agreed to by the Astana trio (Russia, Iran, and Turkey) following the fall of the opposition-held eastern Aleppo in December 2016. The idea of de-escalation was designed - or at least that was the general perception at the time - to freeze the conflict, decrease human suffering, and pave the way for a political solution.

That proved to be a mere illusion. Lacking adequate manpower to fight at different fronts, the Russians threw their weight behind the de-escalation zones idea, originally proposed by the UN special envoy to Syria Staffan de Mistura in 2014.

In addition, following the defeat of the Islamic State of Iraq and the Levant (ISIL, known as ISIS) in Mosul, the Russians started to realize that while they were busy fighting the opposition along the

---

[53] **The Heads of State and Government of the Federative Republic of Brazil, the Russian Federation, the Republic of India, the People's Republic of China and the Republic of South Africa, met from 25 - 27 July 2018 in Johannesburg, at the 10th BRICS Summit. The 10th BRICS Summit, as a milestone in the history of BRICS, was held under the theme "BRICS in Africa: Collaboration for Inclusive Growth and Shared Prosperity in the Fourth Industrial Revolution" focusing on the threat of a US-led global trade war.**
The BRICS group, comprising more than 40 percent of the global population, represents some of the biggest emerging economies.

western belt of Syrian territories between Aleppo and Damascus, the US-backed Syria Democratic Forces (SDF) was quickly retrieving ISIL territories in the oil and gas-rich east.

For that reason, Moscow decided to freeze the conflict with the Syrian opposition and entered into a race with the US-led coalition to regain as much territory from retreating ISIL as possible. The Euphrates River acted as a natural borderline between the Russian and the American spheres of influence.

As the war with ISIL was approaching its end, Russia reverted back to its strategy of crushing the armed opposition before any political solution can be negotiated. It attacked and took over the de-escalation zone in Eastern Ghouta, near the capital, Damascus.

Russia and regime forces then moved onto the province of Homs in the north before going after Deraa and Quneitra n the southwest, near the borders with the Israeli-occupied Golan Heights.

Hundreds of thousands of opposition fighters have been relocated to the northwest under evacuation agreements. Idlib was turned into a gathering place for all opposition factions, along with some two million refugees, preparing for a final showdown.

Shortly after the armed opposition groups were forced to evacuate from the southwest, Syrian President Bashar Al-Assad indicated that Idlib would be his next target.

The Syrian army started to amass troops and drop leaflets over the province, urging people to return to "state rule" and demanding the surrender of the armed factions. However, Idlib looks like a much more complicated case to deal with in political, military and humanitarian terms than the other three de-escalation zones.

With an area of 6,000 square km, De Mistura claimed that there are 2.9 million civilians in the area. That number is nonsense. In 2011 Idlib governorate had a population of 1.5 million. The UN has warned that an offensive in the area could force 2.5 million of them towards the Turkish border and precipitate a massive humanitarian crisis. As for the number of terrorists in Idlib de Mistura only spoke of some 10,000 of the al-Qaeda aligned Hayat Tahrir al-Sham (HTS), the former Jabhat Al-Nusra Front. But the total number of radical Jihadists in the governorate is much larger.

The presence of the al-Qaeda-affiliated Hay'et Tahrir al-Sham (HTS) further complicates the situation. With more than 12,000 fighters, HTS controls a great part of Idlib and has vowed to fight to the end. Plus 10-20,000 Chinese Uyghur jihadists. To the Syrian government, Idlib's "rebels" are all terrorists pure and simple.

Russia, Iran and the Syrian regime use this as a pretext to attack, citing UNSC resolutions, which have designated HTC a terror group.

In addition, Turkey has troops at 12 observation posts in the Idlib province to monitor the Astana truce. Turkey has already warned that an attack on Idlib could put the last nail in the coffin of the Astana process. Turkey and Russia engaged in extensive diplomatic talks to prevent this from happening.

Turkey and Russia have both announced that the leaders of the two countries will hold a bilateral meeting on the sidelines of the Tehran summit to discuss the future of Idlib. Three scenarios can be discussed here.

The first one is that Turkey and Russia would agree to uphold the de-escalation zone in Idlib, providing that Turkey deal with the HTS problem. Turkey tried to persuade the HTS to dissolve itself and melt within the Turkey-backed Free Syrian Army factions.

The HTS foreign fighters have been offered a safe exit to relocate somewhere else. These efforts have not yielded the desired results.

If Turkey fails to deal with the HTS, the second scenario becomes very probable. It would allow for a limited Russian-led military action in Idlib to take out the HTS and other "radical" groups. Given the high population density in the area, Russia and even the Syrian regime seem to be trying to avoid a massive military attack - something that Iran would like to undertake.

At this stage, Russia seems to be mainly seeking to secure its Hmeimim airbase in Latakia from drone attacks by pushing the opposition factions in Idlib further north. The Syrian regime, on the other hand, seems to be mainly interested in regaining control of the M5 highway, the country's main trade road, which passes through parts of Idlib.

For the past two years, the regime's offensive strategy has traced the M5's 470km from Aleppo in the north to Hama, Homs, Damascus and more recently Deraa in the south. The only remaining part of the M5 outside regime control lies now in parts of Idlib.

Indeed, the regime would want to regain every inch of Idlib but simply does not have the manpower to do so, especially against tens of thousands of die-hard opposition elements, with nowhere else to go.

The third and the most feared scenario is an all-out offensive in Idlib. This scenario is unlikely at this stage because it is very costly both politically and militarily. It would also lead to a humanitarian disaster, a massive refugee crisis and destruction at a large scale. It would destroy the evolving partnership between Russia and Turkey and lead to the collapse of the Astana process.

It will put more pressure on the already strained Russian-European relations as it would lead to a new wave of refugees. The US has also warned against a massive attack in Idlib and stated that it would intervene in case chemical weapons are used.

Lastly, an all-out attack in Idlib runs counter to the new Russian strategy, aiming at returning the Syrian refugees back home and starting the reconstruction process with aid from Europe and the Gulf states.

The Tehran summit will, however, show which of these three scenarios will prevail and whether the future of Idlib will be decided by war or by diplomacy.

There is, in fact, some room for cautious optimism here but that is mainly because of war fatigue, not because we have some great diplomats handling the Syrian conflict.

The Trilateral Tehran Summit

As the long-fought Syrian war gradually approaches its ultimate conclusion, Iran, Turkey and Russia seek to guarantee the elimination of militants waging a rebellion against Assad's rule.

Idlib Governate, in Syria, is by far the most-pro-jihadist region in Syria, and has increasingly been collecting jihadists from abroad, for jihadists globally to overthrow and replace Syria's secular Government. Syria is the nation that, for more than seven years, has experienced an influx of jihadists from not only the Arab world, and not only from Muslim-majority countries, but from everywhere, including Asia, Europe and the United States, who have come into Syria to overthrow the only non-sectarian government in the entire Middle East. No other Arab country is secular, and is founded upon equal rights for all of its citizens, regardless of religion. Only Syria is. Jihadists therefore especially hate its government.

On September 7, 2018, Russian President Vladimir Putin, Iranian President Hassan Rouhani and Turkish President Recep Tayyip Erdogan met in Tehran hosted by Iran's Hassan Rouhani to decide the situation in Idlib Province in northwestern of Syria.

The three countries are guarantors of the Astana process, a track of negotiations launched after

Russia's game-changing 2015 military intervention which has eclipsed the Western-backed Geneva negotiations led by the UN.

Iranian and Russian support for Syrian President Bashar al-Assad has shored up the Damascus regime, allowing it to regain the upper hand in the seven-year civil war.

Seized from government forces in 2015, Idlib and adjacent areas form the final major chunk of Syrian territory still under opposition control. Regime backers Russia and Iran have sworn to wipe out terrorists and Assad has declared his determination to retake control of the entire country.

"The illegal presence and interference of America in Syria which has led to the continuation of insecurity in that country, must end quickly," and both Erdogan and Rouhani condemned the alleged US support to rebel groups battling President Bashar al Assad's regime in a conflict that has claimed the lives of at least 5,00,000 people and displaced millions of Syrians, triggering a much larger migrant crisis impacting European nations across the Mediterranean, and the Russian President Putin emphasized that the numerous civilians living in Idlib province must be taken into account before executing any plan to bring about a solution to the conflict and he opposed ceasefire proposal in Idlib. Russia has said the Syrian army is preparing to solve the problem of terrorism in the rebel stronghold and reiterated that its position had not changed.

Iranian President Hassan Rouhani stated that the battle in Syria will prevail until militant transnational jihadists, mainly the 10 to 20 Chinese Uyghurs, are pushed out of the entire country, especially in Idlib, but also underlined that any military operation should avoid civilian casualties. *"The fires of war and bloodshed in Syria are reaching their end,"* Rouhani said, while adding that terrorism must *"be uprooted in Syria, particularly in Idlib."* While the Russian foreign ministry spokeswoman Maria Zakharova said that *"A total and definitive liquidation of the terrorists across all of Syria's territory is necessary."* She stressed however that *"Moscow is doing everything in its power to ensure that human losses and harm to Idlib's civilian population is limited as much as possible."* Her Iranian counterpart, Bahram Ghassemi, assured Damascus of Tehran's support and willingness to *"continue its role as adviser and help"* for the Idlib campaign.

Russia and Iran reclaimed liberating Idlib is vital to complete military victory in Syrian conflict after Syrian troops recaptured nearly all other prominent areas.

The three leaders have jointly agreed to explore options to resolve the situation in Idlib in the next round of Syria talks scheduled to be held in Russia.

On the other side, President Trump [54] tweeted his warning to Syria, as well as its allied Russian and Iranian forces, *"to not launch a military offensive to retake control of the northwest province of Idlib. The area is the last remaining stronghold of illegally armed militant groups in Syria. It's potentially the endgame to the nearly eight-year war".* He also said, *"President Bashar al-Assad of Syria must not recklessly attack Idlib Province. The Russians and Iranians would be making a grave humanitarian mistake to take part in this potential human tragedy."*

---

[54] **Finian Cunningham, *"False-Flag Failure… US Cuts to the Chase to Defend Its Terrorists in Syria",* RT News, September 7, 2018**

The Fourth Sochi Summit

On February 15, 2019, Russia, Turkey, and Iran held their fourth round of talks on Syria in the Russian town of Sochi. Russia insists that Turkey take control of the Al-Qaeda group Hay'et Tahrir al-Sham [55] in the northwestern Syria province of Idlid.

During the summit Russia and Turkey agreed to take "decisive measures" against Hay'et Tahrir al-Sham. Russia and Turkey had previously agreed to create a demilitarized zone around the Idlib province. Hay'et Tahrir al-Sham has violated this agreement and has taken control over most of the demilitarized zone. Turkey has now agreed to clear Hay'et Tahrir al-Sham from the Idlib province.

Turkey has agreed to fight against Hay'et Tahrir al-Sham, Turkey is also trying to bring them into the Turkish controlled "Syrian National Army". The Syrian National Army is a collection of Al-Qaeda groups in Idlib under Turkish leadership.

Here are the main points that came out of this latest Sochi summit. Russia wants Turkey to defeat the Hay'et Tahrir al-Sham (Al-Nusra) Al-Qaeda group in Idlib. Turkey wants to expel Kurdish fighters from northeastern Syria. Turkey wants to wait until the US pulls its troops out of northeastern Syria. Russia and Iran say that the Syrian government should control northeastern Syria.

The Reconstruction projects

Before I start this section, I would like to explain the confusion between the legal terms, "the decree" and "legislative decree". Although they are generally defined as laws, they vary according to the issuing authority. The law is passed by the Parliament or the People's Assembly after discussion. However, the legislative decree is issued by the President of the Republic in special cases, when the People's Assembly is out of session. The legislative decree and the law are equally important, for the decree can amend the laws, and the laws can amend the legislative decrees. The decree is issued by the Presidency and concerns administrative affairs.

Back in September 2012, as the war dragged on, the Syrian government eventually zeroed in on the area for reconstruction plans, President al-Assad signed legislative decree (66/2012) to "*redevelop areas of unauthorized housing and informal settlements, farmland and informal housing in some places within walking distance of central Damascus.*" Construction has begun in the Basateen el-Razi district in southwestern Damascus, under a government development plan which was featured prominently on the Damascus governorate official website, along with conceptual drawings and architectural documents highlighting the project's intended goal.

"*It's important to recognize where the early protest movement started: in the disadvantaged rural areas and these slums, these informal settlements, spreading around the major cities, … The levels of repression in those communities was so much stronger, as well. It was the working-class communities around Damascus that were put under siege very early on… [something that] wasn't happening in the more middle-class areas*" explained Robin Yassin-Kassab and Leila al-Shami in their book "*Burning*

---

[55] **Hay'et Tahrir al-Sham was previously known as Al-Nusra front and is the Syrian affiliate of Al-Qaeda. Hay'et Tahrir al-Sham is considered to be a radical rebel group. It is not a natural enemy of Turkey. Hay'et Tahrir al-Sham served as security guards for the Turkish Army when the Turkish Army first entered the Idlib province.**

Country: Syrians in Revolution and War" [56] which is a vivid and groundbreaking look at a modern-day political and humanitarian nightmare.

In May 2015, President Bashar al-Assad issued a presidential decree (Decree 19) allowing administrative units, including governorates and municipalities, to establish their own private investment companies.

In January 2016, the government passed the Public Private Partnership (PPP) law, six years after it was originally drafted, authorizing the private sector to manage and develop state assets in all sectors of the economy, except for oil. This privatization model is part of the Syrian government's new economic strategy, named the National Partnership, launched in February 2016, to replace the social market economic model developed prior to the uprising.

The "Marouta City" Project

Some of the redevelopment under Decree 66 has been directly transplanted from a 2007 urban plan for Damascus that was still to be implemented when the Syrian uprising erupted in 2011.

For decades, the impoverished residents of southwestern Damascus' Basateen el-Razi district have lived in poorly built shacks and ramshackle housing facing the upscale Mezzeh district, one of the wealthiest areas of Syria. The Basateen el-Razi district comprises mostly informal settlements, locally referred to as "ashwai" [random] zones, that were set up with no official licensing or planning from the state. Therefore, and according to the governorate of Damascus, the new project will tear down old, poorly constructed dwellings to develop an upscale area called "Marouta City." The 2.15 million square meter (531 acre) development will include 12,000 housing units for "an estimated 60,000 residents. The development will include schools, restaurants, mosques, a car park, a shopping mall and at least three 50-floor skyscrapers.

Despite criticism, the Syrian government has moved forward with plans to redevelop the neighborhood, while providing little compensation to residents. Decree 66 has since 2012 provided the legal and financial foundation for reconstruction in several areas returned to Syrian government control, and rebuilding work started in the devastated country in one corner of southwestern Damascus based on the urban planning blueprint President Bashar al-Assad.

In March 2016, President al-Assad inaugurated the multi-million-dollar urban redevelopment project, promising grand designs and a brilliant future for the capital. Armed with planning documents full of futuristic tower blocks, park boulevards, and row upon row of modern-fronted housing.

In February 2017, the governorate of Damascus posted an announcement offering residents of the area nine days – between February 11 and 20 – to apply for "alternative housing" to replace their homes that are to be demolished for the project. The first building permits for the Marouta City project were issued in March 2017. The exact date of demolition was not immediately clear but construction was moving quickly.

As of January 13, 2018, satellite photos of the area from Google Maps shows that foundations have already been built in the Marouta City area. Additionally, a number of roundabouts under construction serve to connect the development to major intersections near Fayez Mansour street and the Beirut Highway.

---

[56] **Robin Yassin-Kassab and Leila Al-Shami *"Burning Country: Syrians in Revolution and War"* – Paperback – February 15, 2016, ISBN-10:0745337821**

The project has also attracted some sizable investments. The Marouta City project is managed chiefly by the Syrian regime, under an organization established and owned by the governorate of Damascus specifically that project, Cham Holdings. Rami Makhlouf, Assad's cousin and one of the wealthiest businessmen in Syria, is a majority shareholder in Cham Holdings, and reportedly recently became involved in the Marouta project, according to the Syria Report. Private investors have invested hundreds of millions of dollars into Marouta City through Damascus Cham Holdings.

Damascus Cham Holdings also received a number of private Syria-based companies – including Talas Group, producer of the Tolido brand, whose food products are very popular among consumers in Jordan, Egypt and Iraq.

On January 14, 2018 Talas Group signed on as a minority shareholder to a joint investment with Damascus Cham Holdings to establish Mirza Company, which will develop 60,000 square meters (14.83 acres) of land in Marouta City with an investment of 23 billion Syrian Lira (pound) - roughly $45 million.

On February 8, 2018 Damascus Cham Holdings announced it would also partner with Al Baraka Bank and a number of other banks in Syria to establish a real estate financing company to fund complete development of Marouta City.

Local authorities across Syria have been treating Decree 66 as a green light for their own reconstruction projects, using the powers invested in a separate May 2016 proclamation to establish their own investment companies – like Damascus Sham – to fund them.

Decree No. 10 of 2018

Law No. 10 of 2018, passed by the Syrian government on April 2, 2018, allowing for creating redevelopment zones across Syria that will be designated for reconstruction and for the establishment of one or more regulatory zones within the general organizational chart of the administrative units or reformulation of organizational plans. The Syrian government is keen for displaced Syrians to return to their hometowns and to provide all necessary facilitations to those who wish to return.

Such a law will create new administrative units within the area that is already organized and registered for many years in the Syrian land registry. Property regulation was necessary to restore the rights of the owners.

Property owners have 30 days to submit documents proving ownership to local authorities. If the required documentation is unavailable, residents or owners can make a case within the 30-day period to the local authorities using other evidence. They must provide the property location, boundaries, and information about the shares they own, and the real estate category the property comes under (commercial or residential), as well as information about any lawsuits they have brought or outstanding suits against them.

If Syrian properties do not appear on the list, people who own property in the zone are to be notified and have 30 days to provide proof of ownership. If they fail to do so, they will not be compensated, and ownership reverts to the province, town, or city where the property is located. Those who succeed in proving property ownership will get shares in the zone.

If the owner is unable to personally make a claim, certain relatives or a designated agent can come forward in their place. Relatives must show that owners cannot personally make the claim. In addition, legally recognized agents must both be appointed by the property owners and require clearance by a government security services, and relatives must prove their relationship to the owner.

But as reported [57] *"Law 10 came into effect in April 2018 as the army was on the brink of crushing the last insurgent enclaves near Damascus, consolidating President Bashar al-Assad's grip over nearly all of western Syria. The law has yet to be applied. … One of big concerns with the law is that it gave people just 30 days to stake ownership claims once an area is designated for redevelopment, according to rights activists and aid groups. Syrian Foreign Minister Walid al-Mualem said on Saturday this time period had been extended to one year.*

Under the law, everyone residing in these zones must move out. Local authorities will provide compensation equivalent to two years' rent to tenants who do not qualify for alternative housing. Tenants who have a right to alternative housing will be placed in that housing within four years, and in the interim will also have their annual rent paid.

Syrian legal experts say the law focuses on war-damaged areas around Damascus and does not include areas undamaged by conflict.

The current Law No. 10 complements Decree 66. However, it includes all of the Syrian territory, for it provides for the establishment of one or more regulatory zones within the overall organizational chart of the administrative units commissioned by the Ministry of Local Administration. These units are able to choose any area and impose a new organizational chart for it, without consulting local councils.

China' Stabilization Strategy in Syria

Though tensions continued to explode between the numerous factions present on Syrian soil, in the major population centers away from the fighting the thoughts of Syria's leaders and their allies were turning towards rebuilding the country's shattered cities and putting Syria's war-damaged economy back on its feet.

For Syria, stabilization should focus on reestablishing a safe and secure environment and providing essential governmental services, emergency infrastructure reconstruction, and humanitarian relief. The effort should be complementary to counterterrorism and a necessary condition for political reconciliation.

For example, Chinese companies have already shown interest in the reconstruction and on January 24, 2017, the Syrian Minister of Transport discussed with Chinese economic delegation ways to promote cooperation in the fields of air transport, ground transport, and railway construction.

Wang Jin [58] wrote: *"Economically, China has the economic capability to help and to play a major role in the post-Syrian-war construction. Under the One Belt, One Road (OBOR) initiative put forward by Chinese leader Xi Jinping in 2013, China's economic expansion abroad has increased significantly. Many Chinese state-owned enterprises have purchased companies from and invested in different foreign states, demonstrating China's economic ambitions. Meanwhile, China has established several international organizations, such as Asian Infrastructure Investment Bank (AIIB), in the hope of reforming the existing international economic system. With China expanding both its economic and political ambitions abroad, taking a leading role in Syria seems like a golden opportunity. The massive amount of foreign currency*

---

[57] **Reuter's reporting on June 4, 2018 from Beirut, Lebanon**
[58] **Wang Jin, "*Will China Pay for Syria to Rebuild?*" The Diplomat, [the international current-affairs magazine for the Asia-Pacific region], February 16, 2017.**

reserves (more than $3 trillion) held by China seems enough to cover the expenses needed for post-Syrian war reconstruction"

Syria sits at the crossroads of branches of China's Silk Road [59] initiative, and provides the most direct land route to China's energy and resource investments in the Gulf and Africa. Because of these past and potential investments, Beijing also has an economic interest in stabilizing Syria and the region and possibly in military and counter-terrorism partnerships with Damascus, Tehran, and Moscow.

China sees a double opportunity in rebuilding the war-torn country: to extend its new Silk Road and expand its economic and political influence westward.

Rising superpower China has stepped forwards to Syria's Bashar al-Assad regime to rebuild and fund Syria's reconstruction efforts. China has also sent Chinese special forces to Syria to help the regime there fight against rebel remnants.

Chinese money and reconstruction aid came to play an increasingly important part in Syria's internal politics, a significant change from before the war. It was reported that Chinese-Syrian negotiations over trade and investment expanded from early diplomatic exchanges to commitments of nearly $2 billion in reconstruction contracts. China has become Syria's largest trade partner, snapping up 80 percent of its export.

China has traditionally avoided diplomatic entanglements there, so this support for Assad marks a shift in regional diplomacy that Chinese diplomats started to enjoy.

By working through the internationally recognized government of Syria, China was able to claim that it has avoided taking sides in a war but has engaged with a sovereign state of Syria's reconstruction support.

What is important to remember that Syria provides the most direct land route to China's energy and resource investments in the Gulf and Africa. Because of these past and potential investments, China also has an economic interest in stabilizing Syria and the region — and possibly in military and counter-terrorism partnerships with Damascus, Tehran, and Moscow.

China is poised to win substantial contracts and to expand its economic influence westward. On May 8, 2018, the China-Arab Research Center on Reform and Development in Beijing organized a Symposium focused on the reconstruction process in Syria and the role that China can play in this domain.

Iran' Stabilization Strategy in Syria

The Islamic Republic of Iran has strong relations with Syria and has stood by it in facing all challenges. The deep, strategic and historic relations between the people of Syria and Iran is not shaken by any force in the world. Iran has solidified its position in Syria as President Assad remained in place. It is virtually impossible to imagine reconstruction in Syria without Iranian involvement.

Iran has sent Syria vast quantities of military equipment throughout the civil war, including rifles, machine guns, ammunition, mortar shells, and other arms, as well as military communications equipment.

The Iranian regime's support for Syria is broad and comprehensive and its efforts to cement its role in Syria has regional implications.

---

[59] **The Silk Road was an ancient network of trade routes that connected the East and West. It was central to cultural interaction between them for centuries.**

Iran's assistance has been critical in keeping Assad in power, even as the international community has sought to put an end him. Iran was also instrumental in transforming the Syrian Civil War into a regional sectarian battle against terrorism rather than against the fabricated uprising against the Assad regime. The assistance from Iran has kept Assad in power long enough for Russian intervention to turn the tide of the battle in his favor. Particularly after the victories Iran gave Assad in Aleppo and the success of the campaign into Badiyat al-Sham, the Syrian President was less inclined to provide concessions to opposition forces.

It was reported [60] recently that during a visit to Damascus by Iran's First Vice President Eshaq Jahangiri, Syria and Iran signed 11 agreements and memoranda of understanding including a "long-term strategic economic cooperation" deal aimed at strengthening cooperation between Damascus and Iran. The agreements covered a range of fields including economy, culture, education, infrastructure, investment and housing.

The agreements included two memos of understanding between the railway authorities of the two countries as well as between their respective investment promotion authorities.

In relation to infrastructure, there was also rehabilitation of the ports of Tartus and Latakia as well as construction of a 540-megawatt energy plant. In addition, there were "dozens of projects in the oil sector and agriculture".

The illegal world war in Syria has taken an enormous toll on the Syrian economy and infrastructure, with the cost of war-related destruction estimated by the UN at about $400 billion.

No doubt that Iran stands alongside Syria during the next phase that will be marked by reconstruction.

These agreements come against the backdrop of fresh US sanctions against Iran, while Syrian President Bashar al-Assad's regime and several Syrian businesspeople and companies are already on US and European blacklists. They also come as Israel has repeatedly pledged to keep arch-foe Iran from entrenching itself militarily in Syria.

Russia' Stabilization Strategy in Syria

Russia has become increasingly clear that what's good for the Syrian government is also good for Russia. Russian air and artillery support have enabled the regime's most important advances.

Records show that Russian defense industry contracts with Syria exceed $4 billion with an added $162 million per year in Russian arms sales to Syria in 2009 and 2010. Additionally, Russia holds a $550 million aviation contract with Syria as well as a Tartus naval base contract, which leases the Soviet-era port to the Syrian government for an unspecified price.

Both the Hmeimim air force base and the Tartus naval facility, which is being upgraded to a regular naval base, will stay in place for decades after the end of the war. The Syrian armed forces will continue to rely on Russian weapons and equipment, and Russian military specialists will continue to advise and train their Syrian colleagues. This will seal Syria's role as Russia's main geopolitical and military foothold in the Middle East.

Russia plans to help Syria rebuild energy facilities that have been devastated by years of war, Russian Energy Minister Aleksandr Novak was quoted as saying by Russian news agencies on

---

[60] **Agence France-Presse (AFP), January 29,2019**

February 13, [61]: *"We have signed a road map, not only in the field of electricity but also oil and gas, covering the restoration of oil fields and the development of new deposits."*

As the main international backer of Syrian President Bashar al-Assad, Russia has become deeply involved in helping the war-battered country rebuild as fighting against Syrian Sunni rebels has subsided in recent months.

Another Russian agreement was signed on the *"rehabilitation, modernization, and construction of new energy facilities in Syria."* Russia's Energy Ministry said on its website: *"We attach great importance to restoring the Syrian economy, especially the oil and gas sectors which will certainly contribute to the normalization of the economic and social situation in the country."*

To Russian Deputy Prime Minister Dmitry Rogozin, *"Syria is a land of unlimited riches, … and Russian companies have the moral right to develop large-scale economic projects in Syria."*

As well as a starting step toward reconstruction, it was reported that Russia assembled $1 billion for reconstruction projects in Syria.

Russia Builds Syria's damaged infrastructure

With the war in Syria going on since 2011, the world is noticing that by the year 2018 Syria's damaged infrastructure is being restored with Russian help. Schools and factories have been built up again, school children and factory workers are gradually returning.

Furthermore, thousands of Syrian volunteer organizations provide help and assistance to their countrymen in need. The Indian analyst M.K. Bhadrakumar thinks that "paradoxically, while Middle Eastern politics is in turmoil, the prospects for peace in Syria may have improved. (…) Russia and Iran intend to retain their military footprints in Syria for a foreseeable future"[62].

Furthermore, the Russian News Agency (TASS) reported [63] that the Russian Federation operates a reconciliation center for humanitarian aid in Syria. It gives medical assistance at border crossings because the main efforts of the Russian military are now focused on assistance to the refugees returning to their homes.

The Russian reconciliation center also sends clothing and food to people in need, for example in the city of Aleppo. In November 2018, TASS reported that "humanitarian operations were conducted in the city of Aleppo. A total of 150 school backpacks with school kits were handed out to pupils in the *Fatih Marashi* school in the *Ashaar* neighborhood. As many as 150 outfits and 150 blankets were distributed among civilians in the *Julub* neighborhood. Apart from that, one ton of fresh bread was handed out" [64]

Another humanitarian operation was conducted in the first week of December 2018. Sergei Solomatin, Head of the Russian reconciliation center, reported that 500 bags of food were handed out to residents of *Skalbiya* in the Hama governorate. Apart from that, Russian military is joining Syrians in their efforts to restore infrastructure facilities in Syria. More than 30000 residential

---

[61] **RadioFreeEurope, *"Russia Plans to Help Syria Rebuild Devastated Oil, Power Industries"*** February 14, 2018

[62] **Indian Punchline, November 20,.2018**

[63] **Russian News Agency (TASS), November 30, 2018**

[64] **Russian News Agency (TASS), November 13, 2018.**

houses, 709 educational and 117 medical facilities have been restored. A total of 927 kilometers of motorways have been repaired in Syria up to now [65]

Especially in the city of Aleppo, 130 damaged schools were repaired by the Syrian authorities, and 340 more schools in the eastern part of Aleppo province. Despite the ongoing war, young people need to receive education because they are important for the future of the country and will ensure its survival. A total of 1349 schools are currently open in Aleppo. Some school buildings were almost completely destroyed during the war. Engineer Bassam Makhshur, who works on restoring schools, said that the most difficult part is clearing out debris: *"The most difficult stage is the first stage – clearing out debris. Works were often halted, as we found mines under every collapsed wall, and we had to call in sappers"*[66]

In addition, Syrian children will be able to study at cadet schools of the Russian Defense Ministry for free. The document was signed in Moscow on the 20th of September 2018. It entered into force on the 20th of October 2018. The Syrian children will pursue curricula developed for Russian cadets and receive instruction in the Russian language on a gratuitous basis. Expenses will be paid by the Russian side. In this way, the Russian Federation wants to help build up the Syrian Armed Forces so they can operate on their own in the future.[67]

The Syrian Arab News Agency reported[68] that hundreds of factories have returned to work in Damascus and its countryside. According to Samer Al Debs, Head of the Chamber of Industry in Damascus, 710 factories in Damascus and 90 factories in *Tal Kurdi* are functioning again, along with a number of small handicraft workshops in *Al Sbeine* and *Al Qadam* near Damascus. He explained that the Syrian industry faces great challenges. Laws and regulations are needed, as well as a strategic vision to promote and market Syrian industrial products. Samer Al-Debs pointed out that the situation is getting better as more areas are being restored, not to mention the re-opening of the Nassib border crossing center and starting exports.

The Syrians are very patriotic people. Many civilians are helping the Syrian and the Russian military to restore damaged facilities in Syria. As the Syrian Arab News Agency reported, they are the *"very core of civil society and have an integral role as key partner in community development in the pre-and post-war periods. The concept of voluntary work in Syria has changed in order to alleviate the negative repercussions of the terrorist war waged against the country. Thus, the majority of charity events and societal activities aim to provide support and help to the martyrs' families, the wounded army personnel, women, children, persons with disabilities, the elderlies and displaced families"*[69]

Thousands of Syrian youths took part in different volunteering activities to convey a message that Syria is not giving up. Up to 600 university students benefited from 60 free training hours offered as part of the initiative. Volunteer work has been essential to support Syrian steadfastness against terrorism and war.

In the same context, the war waged on Syria necessitated great efforts to provide support to all Syrians confronted with difficult circumstances. According to a survey conducted by the Syrian Ministry of Social Affairs, there are 1.500 civil and non-governmental volunteer organizations operating in different Syrian provinces. This shows that the Syrians are patriotic and idealistic people, not giving up but fighting for the survival of their nation and state.

---

[65] **Russian News Agency (TASS), December 8, 2018.**

[66] **Russian News Agency (TASS), December 6, 2018.**

[67] **Russian News Agency (TASS), October 30, 2018.**

[68] **Syrian Arab News (SANA) December 4, 2018.**

[69] **Syrian Arab News (SANA) December 5, 2018.**

In short, the Assad government fought back, backed by Russia, Iran and Hezbollah. Syria survived and has reestablished itself. But the United States and its allies refuse to recognize these realities, and so Trump's move to boost Israeli Prime Minister Benjamin Netanyahu's standing by legally recognizing Israel's annexation of the Golan plunges both countries further into dangerous delusion. Trump failed in Syria and will withdraw his troops out of Syria that will allow it to enjoy freedom and independence on all the Syria territories.

The Russia Initiative to help Syrian Refugees Return

In August 2018 more than 90% of the Syrian Territories were stabilized under President Bashar Assad who has recovered control of most of Syria and became really willing to accept all those who want to come back to their homes. Stability in Syria allowed Russia to set up a refugee center in Syria to help refugees return.

Syrians start returning home as they understand that there is no threat from the government and from the governmental security apparatus and they are returning to their homes, to their territories which are now under the control of the government.

Some 5.6 million Syrians are registered as refugees in the region, around 890,000 of them in Lebanon ready to return to Syria, as well as 300,000 from Turkey and 200,000 from European Union countries according to the Russian initiative.

Lebanon expressed readiness to offer the necessary assistance to implement the Russian proposals because the Syrian refugees became an existential threat to Lebanon, and has been calling for their voluntary return to secure areas of Syria before a political settlement to the war.

Lebanon's General Security directorate has worked with Damascus to coordinate the return of hundreds of refugees since the month of June, 2018.

The Reconstruction of Syria

Syria has passed through the crisis stage and entered the reconstruction phase with the plan to Re-build Syria exhibition of 2018.

The Re-Build Syria Exhibition of 2018

From October 2 to October 6, 2018, the "Re-Build Syria" - an International Trade Exhibition - took place at Damascus International Fairgrounds, it was specialized in the following topics:

- Displaying International Agriculture Technologies, Fertilizers, Irrigation Systems, Planting Machines, Tractors, Alternative Energy and other equipment. This event offered the perfect platform to ensure the Rehabilitation of the Soil and the Agriculture fields in Syria, and helped to present the machinery for professional plant production.
- Pioneering in showcasing the true platform for both local and international Real Estate companies and banks to meet with the Businessmen Delegations from across the world and showcase their products and services. The upcoming Real Estate opportunities across major property markets as part of the Syrian growing market for experienced and aspiring

Real Estate investors across the region because at the upcoming phase, qualified and motivated investors met to discuss investment in the real estate domain which had become intensively focused upon by being one of the major sectors of the rebuilding process through its contribution to the national economy and development. It is a unique platform to escalate business networking through Banking Services, top executives, the regional and international investors, developers, investment promotion authorities and other Real Estate professionals to drive growth in Real Estate investment and development across emerging markets globally.

- Exhibiting health showcase that was the most important platform for all medical professionals who exposed their latest and most sophisticated innovation in the medical industry under one roof. Statistics say that over 39% of the Hospitals in Syria were severely damaged during the war, and (over 12% of these hospitals are completely out of service). So, this exhibition aimed at attracting investors and distribute equipment to help provide opportunities from Syria and abroad by showcasing the qualified materials to rebuild and restore the health sector.

- Displaying a showcase for products of Printing, Packaging, plastic and Petrochemicals to provide a qualified audience, potential buyers and business partners across the region, to take the opportunity to open up new fields of business. The goal of the event provided the latest technologies and equipment in the printing, packaging, plastic and petrochemical sectors. This exhibition connected suppliers, distributers, buyers to gain a perspective on the industry that drives innovation at the plant. The exhibitors benefited by distributing their latest technologies, products, services and solutions for all retailers and consumer packaged goods.

- Exhibiting the most effective and cutting-edge technologies and product services to meet the requirement of the Syrian growing market. This exhibition brought together local and International exhibitors, manufacturers, distributors, security and technology professionals and end users to connect and create unparalleled business opportunities.

- Exhibiting Syrian stone is an essential element in construction, for its strength, and beauty of form which contributes to increase the aesthetic value of the building process. Stone takes 20% of the building process or even more if it is made of marble, ceramic or natural stone. All the projects existing in Syria whether it is for restorations, repairs or building projects have been taking stone as an essential element in construction for its beauty and durability.

In short, Syria's realities on the ground is best described by President Bashar Al-Assad as follows:

Dr Bashar Al-Assad description of the realities on the Syrian ground

Dr. Bashar Al-Assad, the President of the Syrian Arab Republic gave a long and detailed interview[70] clarifying the situation in Syria by insisting that the Russian-Turkish agreement on northern Syria is

---

[70] **The Syrian TV and the Syrian Al-Ikhbaria TV and was published by the Syrian Arab news Agency (SANA) on October 31, 2019**

temporal, and it curbs the Turkish excess to achieve more damage through occupying more Syrian territories and cut the road in front of the US.

President Al-Assad affirmed that the entrance of the Syrian Arab Army into regions of northern Syria is an expression of the entrance of the Syrian State with all services it offers, adding that the army has reached the majority of the regions, but not completely. The President underlined that Syria hasn't offered any concessions regarding the formation of the committee of discussing the constitution.

Concerning Turkey

To Al-Assad, these realities on the ground have achieved two things; the withdrawal of armed groups from the north to the south in coordination with the Syrian Army, and as such the advance of the Syrian Army to the north, to the area not occupied by the Turks.

These two elements are positive, but they do not cancel out the negative aspects of the Turkish presence until they are driven out one way or another. This agreement is a temporary one, not permanent. If Syrians take for example the de-escalation areas at a certain period of time, some people believed that they were permanent and that they will give terrorists the right to remain in their areas indefinitely. The fact was that it was an opportunity to protect civilians, and also to talk to the terrorists with the objective of driving them out later. So, we have to distinguish between ultimate or strategic goals on the one hand, and tactical approaches on the other.

Al-Assad added that in the short term, it is a good agreement – and he explains why; the Turkish incursion, not only reflects Turkey's territorial greed but also expresses American desire. The Russian relationship with Turkey is positive. On the other hand, it outmaneuvers the American game in the north. Such as the recent German proposal which was immediately supported by NATO – and the Germans would not make this except on behalf of the Americans, NATO is the same thing as America. The proposal talked about restoring security to this region under international auspices. This means that the area would be outside the control of the Syrian state and thus making separation a reality on the ground. Through this agreement, the Russians reigned in the Turks, outmaneuvered the Americans and aborted the call for internationalization which was proposed by the Germans. That is why this agreement is a positive step. It does not achieve everything, in the sense that it will not pressure the Turks to leave immediately. However, it limits the damage and paves the way for the liberation of this region in the future, or the immediate future.

To President Bashar, there is no Turkish army, in the technical sense in Idlib. But we are in one arena, the whole Syrian arena is one – a single theatre of operations. From the furthest point in the south to the furthest point in the north Turkey is the American proxy in this war, and everywhere we have fought we have been fighting this proxy. So, when he does not leave after we exhaust every possible means, there won't be any other choice but war, this is self-evident. The President says that in the near future we must give room to the political process in its various forms. If it does not yield results then this is an enemy and you go to war against it; there is no other choice.

While in Idlib, President Bashar agrees that there is an agreement through the Astana Process that the Turks will leave. The Turks did not abide by this agreement, but we are liberating Idlib. There was a delay for a year; the political process, the political dialogue, and various attempts were given an opportunity to drive the terrorists out. All possibilities were exhausted. In the end, we liberated areas gradually through military operations. The same will apply in the northern region after exhausting all political options.

To Al-Assad, we must remember that Erdogan aimed, from the beginning of the war, to create a problem between the Syrian people and the Turkish people, to make it an enemy, which will happen through a military clash. At the beginning of the war, the Turkish Army supported the Syrian Army and cooperated with us to the greatest possible extent, until Erdogan's coup against the Army. Therefore, we must continue in this direction, and ensure that Turkey does not become an enemy state. Erdogan and his group are enemies, because he leads these policies, but until now most of the political forces in Turkey are against Erdogan's policies; and that Erdogan is as a thief, and from the first days he started stealing everything related to Syria. So, he is a thief. I was not calling him names; I was describing him. This is an adjective and this description is true. What do you call somebody who steals factories, crops and finally land? A benefactor? He is a thief, there is no other name. Previously in my speech before the People's Assembly, I said that he is a political thug. He exercises this political thuggery on the largest scale. He lies to everyone, blackmails everyone. He is a hypocrite and publicly so. We are not inventing an epithet; he declares himself through his true attributes. So, I only described him.

If you are asking me how would I feel if I, personally, had to shake hands with a person from the Erdogan group, or someone of similar leanings or who represents his ideology – I would not be honored by such a meeting and I would feel disgusted. But we have to put our personal feelings aside when there is a national interest at stake. If a meeting would achieve results, I would say that everything done in the national interest should be done. This is the responsibility of the state. I do not expect a meeting to produce any results unless circumstances change for the Turks. And because the Erdogan-type Turks are opportunists and belong to an opportunist organization and an opportunist ideology, they will produce results according to changing circumstances, when they are under pressure, depending on their internal or external circumstances or maybe their failure in Syria. Then, they might produce results.

But we must ensure not to turn Turkey into an enemy, and here comes the role of friends – the Russian role and the Iranian role. Russia accepted the Turkish incursion, or that Russia wanted to turn a blind eye in the fact that. In fact, it is not true. For over a year, the Russians were concerned about the seriousness of such a proposition. We all knew that the Turkish proposition was serious, but it was shackled by American orders or desires. Some people might criticize the Russians for this outcome, due to their position at the United Nations.

As I said a short while ago, the President continues, the Russians deal with realities on the ground, consequently, they try to ensure that all political conditions are in place in order to pave the way for their departure from Syria and limit the damage by the Turks or reign in the Turkish recalcitrance aimed at inflicting more damage and occupying more land. But the Russians were certainly not part of this agreement – Russian agreements are always public. The Russian-Turkish agreement was announced immediately, with all its items; the agreement between us and the Kurds, with Russian mediation.

Concerning Turkey and Israel

The difference between Turkey and Israel, according to President Al-Assad, is that we do not recognize the legitimacy of Israel existence as a state. We don't recognize the existence of the Israeli people. There are no Israeli people except the one that existed for several centuries BC, now they are a diaspora who came and occupied land and evicted its people. While the Turkish people exist, and they are a neighboring people, and we have a common history, regardless of whether this history is good or bad or in between; that is irrelevant. Turkey exists as a state and it is a neighboring state. The Alexandretta issue is different from the situation in which a people without land replace a land and a people; the comparison is not valid. Even when we negotiated with Israel in the 1990s, we did not recognize it. We negotiated in order to achieve peace. If this was achieved and the rights were returned, we would recognize it; as I said, the comparison is invalid. Turkey will continue to exist and the Turks should remain a brotherly people. Erdogan was betting at the beginning to mobilize the Turkish people behind him in order to create hostility with the Syrian people, and consequently be given a free hand. We have to be careful not to look at things in the same way. I stress again that some people, not the political forces, but within the Turkish Army and security institutions are against Erdogan. This was the reason behind our drive to meet them.

Concerning Israel, we fight the Israelis' agents, flunkies or tools, in different ways, some military some political. They are all tools serving Israel directly or through the Americans. Since the battle on the ground is with these forces, it is normal that the terminology describes these forces and not Israel. Israel is in fact a main partner in what is happening, and as an enemy state, that is expected. Will it stand by and watch? No. it will be proactive, and more effective in order to strike at Syria, the Syrian people, the Syrian homeland and everything related to Syria.

Concerning the United States

Al-Assad said: The reality is that the Americans are occupiers, whether they are in the east, the north or the south, the result is the same. Once again, we should not be concerned with Trump's statements, but rather deal with the reality. When we are finished with the areas according to our military priorities and we reach an area in which the Americans are present, the President Bashar will not go to indulge in heroics and say that we will send the army to face the Americans. *"We are talking about a super power. Do we have the capabilities to do that? I believe that this is clear for us as Syrians. Do we choose resistance? If there is resistance, the fate of the Americans will be similar to their fate in Iraq. But the concept of resistance needs a popular state of mind that is the opposite of being agents and proxies, a patriotic popular state which carries out acts of resistance. The natural role of the state in this case is to provide all the necessary conditions and necessary support to any popular resistance against the occupier."*

Bashar made it clear as a right solution that if we put to one side the colonial and commercial American mentality which promotes the colonization of certain areas for money, oil and other resources, we must not forget that the main agents which brought the Americans, the Turks and others to this region are Syrians acting as agents of foreigners – Syrian traitors. Dealing with all the other cases is just dealing with the symptoms, while we should be addressing the causes. We should be dealing with those Syrians and try to reformulate the patriotic state of the Syrian society – to restore patriotism, restore the unity of opinion and ensure that there are no Syrian traitors. To ensure that all Syrians are patriots, and that treason is no longer a matter of opinion, a mere difference over a political issue. We should all be united against occupation. When we reach this state, I assure you that the Americans will leave on their own accord because they will have no opportunity to remain in Syria; although America is a superpower, it will not be able to remain in Syria. This is something we saw in Lebanon at a certain point and in Iraq at a later stage.

As for Trump, you might ask me a question and *"I give you an answer that might sound strange. I say that the billionaire real estate magnate is the best American president, not because his policies are good, but because he is the most transparent president."* Al-Assad added: "All American presidents perpetrate all kinds of political atrocities and all crimes and yet still win the Nobel Prize and project themselves as defenders of human rights and noble and unique American values, or Western values in general. The reality is that they are a group of criminals who represent the interests of American lobbies, i.e. the large oil and arms companies, and others. Trump talks transparently, saying that what we want is oil. This is the reality of American policy, at least since WWII. We want to get rid of such and such a person or we want to offer a service in return for money. This is the reality of American policy. What more do we need than a transparent opponent? That is why the difference is in form only, while the reality is the same."

By the way, at this point I would like to quote part of Trump remarks [71] saying that his decision was about drawing a line under America's "endless wars" in pursuit of regime change overseas but enacting it brought him into conflict. "We're keeping the oil – remember that." I've always said that: "Keep the oil." We want to keep the oil. Forty-five million dollars a month? Keep the oil. We've secured the oil."

Concerning the Kurds in Syria

What happened during this war is a distortion of concepts; to say that this group of Kurds has a certain characteristic, negative or positive, is neither objective nor rational. It is also unpatriotic. Among the Kurds there were people who were American agents or proxies. This is true, but among the Arabs there were similar cases in the Jazeera area and in other areas in Syria. This applies to most segments of Syrian society. The mistake which was made was that this action was made by a group of Kurds who made themselves representatives, not only of the Kurds, but of the Arabs and others segments of society in Al-Jazeera region. The Americans, through their support with weapons and money – of course the money is not American, it comes from some gulf Arab states – helped establish the authority of these groups over all segments of the society, leading us to believe that those in the area were all Kurds. So, we are actually dealing with the various Kurdish parties. As for the Kurds themselves, most of them had good relations with the Syrian state, and they were always in contact with us and proposed genuine patriotic ideas. In some of the areas we entered, the reaction of the Kurds was no less positive, or less joyful and happy than the reaction of other people there. So, this evaluation is not accurate. Yes, very simply, we can live once again with each other. If the answer were no, it means that Syria will never be stable again.

Concerning Russia and Iran

President Al-Assad made it obvious that: "We, the Russians and the Iranians are involved in the same military battle and the same political battle. We are always in talks with each other to

---

[71] **President Trump's remarks at the International Association of Chiefs of Police Convention in Chicago, Chicago Tribune, October 28, 2019**

determine the circumstances which allow for an operation to go ahead. On several occasions, we agreed on a specific timing for a certain operation, which was later postponed because of military or political developments. This dialogue is normal. There are issues we see on the internal arena, and there are issues seen by Iran on the regional arena and there are those issues seen by the Russians on the international arena. We have an integrated approach based on dialogue. In the past month, I have held five meetings with Russian and Iranian officials, so less than a week apart. Between each two meetings there were military and political developments such that what had been agreed in the first meeting was then changed or modified in the second, third and fourth meetings and the last of which was yesterday. The fast pace of developments makes it necessary sometimes to postpone operations. On the other hand, we have contacts with civilians in those areas. We really try hard to make it possible for civilians to move from those areas into our areas in order to save lives; moreover, if a political solution was possible, and sometimes we succeeded in finding such a solution, it would save the lives of Syrian soldiers, which is a priority that we should not ignore. So, there are many elements, which are difficult to go into now, which affect this decision and postpone it; it is not a matter of pressure. The Russians are as enthusiastic about fighting terrorism as we are, otherwise why would they send their fighter jets? The timing depends on dialogue.

Russia was with us in liberating Khan Skeikhoon and its environs; announcing an end to military operations does not mean an end to fighting terrorism. Indeed, the major battles have almost finished, because most areas either surrender voluntarily or are subject to limited operations. The Khan Sheikhoon operation might look on the map as a major battle, but there was in fact a collapse on the part of the militants. So, maybe this is what was meant by the end of the major operations. Their statements that Idlib should return under the control of the Syrian state and their determination to strike at terrorism have not changed.

Furthermore, and this was the subject of discussion with our Russian and Iranian friends – who said that yes, we are defending you, but in the end, you are the owners of the cause. This is true, the land is ours, and the cause is ours and so we have a duty to carry out by meeting them directly, even if we do not expect results. Maybe there will come a day when we can achieve results, particularly with changing circumstances inside Turkey, in the world and within Syria.

To Al-Assad, he believes that Russian involvement anywhere is in Syrians interest, because the Syrian principles are the same and their battle is one. So, Russian involvement will certainly have positive results. It does not matter whether the Russians are appeasing the Turks or not or whether they are playing a tactical game with them. What is important is the strategy.

Concerning Trump promises to the Turks

The Journalist asked the President about the leader of the dissolved Syrian Democratic Forces, Mazloum Abdi, who made statements to the media in which he said that Trump promised them in an American-Kurdish agreement that before withdrawal he will contact the Russians to find a solution to the Kurdish question by making an agreement with the Russians and the Syrian state to give the Kurds an opportunity to defend themselves.

Al-Assad answers that the Americans whether they say that to an enemy or a friend, the result is the same – it is unreliable. That is why we do not waste our time on things like this. The only Russian agreement with the Kurds was what we talked about in terms of a Russian role in reaching an agreement with Kurdish groups – we should not say with the Kurds, because this is inaccurate and we cannot talk about one segment – the groups which call themselves SDF with the Syrian Army to be deployed. Of course, the Syrian Army cannot be deployed only to carry out purely security or military acts. The deployment of the Syrian Army is an expression of the presence of the Syrian state, which means the presence of all the services which should be provided by the state. This agreement was concluded, and we reached most regions but not completely. There are still obstacles. We intervene because we have direct and old relations – before the Turkish incursion – with these groups. Sometimes they respond, in other places they don't. But certainly, the Syrian Arab Army will reach these areas simultaneously with full public services, which means the return of full state authority. I want to reiterate, that this should take place gradually. Second, the situation will not return as before. There are facts on the ground which need to be addressed, and this will take time. There are new facts related to people on the ground which took place when the state was absent. There are armed groups; we do not expect them to hand over their weapons immediately. Our policy should be gradual and rational, and should take the facts into account. But the ultimate goal is to return to the situation as it used to be previously which is the full control of the state."

President Al-Assad added that I said before whatever the Americans say has no credibility, whether they say that to an enemy or a friend, the result is the same – it is unreliable. American politicians are actually guilty until proven innocent, not the other way around. American politics are no different from Hollywood; it relies on the imagination. Not even science fiction, just mere imagination. So, you can take American politics and see it in Hollywood or else you can bring Hollywood and see it through American politics. The director of the whole scenario is the American policy in the Middle East. And that we should not bet on any American President. First, when Erdogan says that he decided to make an incursion or that they told the Americans, he is trying to project

Turkey as a super power or to pretend that he makes his own decisions; all these are theatrics shared between him and the Americans. In the beginning, nobody was allowed to interfere, because the Americans and the West believed that demonstrations will spread out and decide the outcome. The demonstrations did not spread as they wanted, so they shifted towards using weapons. When weapons did not decide the outcome, they moved towards the terrorist extremist organizations with their crazy ideology in order to decide the outcome militarily. That is why we do not waste our time on things like this. The only Russian agreement with the Kurds was what we talked about in terms of a Russian role in reaching an agreement with Kurdish groups – we should not say with the Kurds, because this is inaccurate and we cannot talk about one segment – the groups which call themselves SDF with the Syrian Army to be deployed. Of course, the Syrian Army cannot be deployed only to carry out purely security or military acts. The deployment of the Syrian Army is an expression of the presence of the Syrian state, which means the presence of all the services which should be provided by the state. This agreement was concluded, and we reached most regions but not completely. There are still obstacles. We intervene because we have direct and old relations – before the Turkish incursion – with these groups. Sometimes they respond, in other places they don't. But certainly, the Syrian Arab Army will reach these areas simultaneously with full public services, which means the return of full state authority.

Al-Assad reiterates that this should take place gradually. Second, the situation will not return as before. There are facts on the ground which need to be addressed, and this will take time. There are new facts related to people on the ground which took place when the state was absent. There are armed groups; we do not expect them to hand over their weapons immediately. Our policy should be gradual and rational, and should take the facts into account. But the ultimate goal is to return to the situation as it used to be previously which is the full control of the state.

Concerning the Armenians in Syria

If we take an example of the latest group which joined the Syrian fabric, the Armenians, President Al-Assad calls the Armenians a patriotic group par excellence. This was proven without a shadow of doubt during the war. At the same time, this group has its own societies, its own churches and more sensitively, it has its own schools. And if you attend any Armenian celebration, a wedding, or any other event – and I used to attend such events because I used to have friends among them previously – they sing their traditional songs but afterwards they sing national, politically-inclined songs. Is there any form of freedom that exceeds this? The Syrian Armenians are the least, among other Armenians of the world, dissolved in society.

They have integrated, but not dissolved into Syrian society. They have maintained all their characteristics. Why should we be open here and unopen with others? The reason is that there are separatist propositions. There are maps showing a Syrian Kurdistan as part of a larger Kurdistan. Now, it is our right to defend our territorial integrity and to be wary of separatist propositions. But we do not have a problem with Syrian diversity. On the contrary, Syrian diversity is rich and beautiful which translates into strength. We do not have an adverse view of this; but richness and diversity are one thing and separating and fragmenting the country is something else, something contrary. That is the problem.

Concerning the Constitution

Al-Assad considers that a large part of the discussion on setting up the constitutional committee is not important: shall we amend the constitution or have a new constitution? Our position was that when we amend a provision of the constitution and put it to a referendum, it becomes a new constitution. So, there is no real difference between amending the constitution or having a new one, because there is nothing to define the new constitution, a completely new constitution. This is all theoretical and has no real meaning. What concerns us is that everything produced by the meetings of this committee and is in line with national interest – even if it is a new constitution from A to Z, we shall approve. And if there is an amendment of a single provision in the constitution, which is against national interest, we would oppose it. So, in order not to waste our time in such sophistry, we should focus on the implications. We are fully aware of the game they are going to play. They aim to weaken the state and transform it into a state which cannot be controlled from within and, consequently is controlled from the outside. The game is clear, as is happening in neighboring countries which we don't need to mention. This is not going to happen; but they will try and we will not accept. This is the summary of months of future dialogue, and maybe longer, I don't know. Of course, I mean future dialogue.

Concerning Security Council Resolution 2254

President Al-Assad considers the constitutional committee of the Security Council Resolution 2254 has the outcomes that might produce later would be used as a launching pad to attack and strike at the structure of the Syrian state. This is what the West has been planning for years, and we know this. That is why it was not an option to concede on fundamentals and particular stances related to Syria's interest. There were other details which were insignificant, like the fact that they camouflaged themselves under the umbrella of the so-called moderate opposition. In many instances, they proposed names affiliated to al-Nusra Front, which we rejected because of this affiliation.

It is said that the meetings of the constitutional committee in Geneva would open the door to reaching a comprehensive solution to the Syrian crisis, as the solution includes holding parliamentary and presidential elections under the supervision of the United Nations and in accordance with Security Council Resolution 2254. He also talked about ensuring the participation of Syrian expatriates. President Bashar does not accept international supervision on parliamentary and presidential elections.

The solution starts by striking at terrorism in Syria. It starts by stopping external interference in Syria. Any Syrian-Syrian dialogue complements, contributes and plays a certain role.

To Al-Assad, supervising the elections means that they are returning to the era of the mandate. I would like to recall that the first part of the resolution refers to Syria's sovereignty, which is expressed by the Syrian state alone and no one else. The elections that will be held will be under the supervision of the Syrian state from A to Z. If we want to invite any other party – an international body, certain states, organizations, societies, individuals or personalities, it will still be under the supervision of the Syrian state and under the sovereignty of the Syrian state. The constitutional committee has nothing to do with the elections it is only tasked with the constitution. If they believe that they will return to the days of the mandate, then that would only be in their dreams.

Al-Assad continues by saying: "to form the constitutional committee is an implied acceptance of the other side and constitutes a joined commitment before the Syrian people to try and agree, under the auspices of the United Nations, on the constitutional arrangements for Syria. Some people objected to this implied acceptance of the other side by the committee, since it does not represent the Syrian people and is not elected by the Syrian people. What is your response to that?

the Syrian government is not part of these negotiations nor of these discussions. But the government supports this because we believe that we share the same viewpoint. They are people who belong to the same political climate of the Syrian government. This does not imply that the government is part of the negotiations. Legally, we are not a part of the constitutional committee and this does not imply the government's recognition of any party; this issue is should be clear.

The return to Geneva only geographically, whereas politically, we are part of Sochi, and everything that is happening has its frame of reference as Sochi and is a continuation of it. There is no Geneva, it is not part of this process. The fact that the UN is represented and participates in Sochi gives it an international dimension, which is necessary; but it does not mean that Geneva undercuts Sochi. There is no Geneva.

Concerning fighting Terrorism

Fighting terrorism is not achieved by theorizing, making rhetorical statements or by preaching. As for postponing, had we waited for an international decision – and by international decision I mean American, British, French and those who stand with them – we would not have liberated any region in Syria since the first days of the war. These pressures have no impact. Sometimes we factor in certain political circumstances; as I said, we give political action an opportunity so that there is no pretext, but when all these opportunities are exhausted, military action becomes necessary in order to save civilians, because I cannot save civilians when they are under the control of the militants. Western logic is an intentionally and maliciously up-side-down logic. It says that the military operation should be stopped in order to protect civilians, whilst for them the presence of civilians under the authority of terrorists constitutes a form of protection for the civilians. The opposite is actually true. The military intervention aims at protecting the civilians, by leaving civilians under the authority of terrorists you extend a service to terrorists and take part in killing civilians.

Concerning Fighting Corruption

President Al-Assad had started fighting corruption before the war, but the circumstances were different before the war, and priorities were different. Now fighting corruption was given priority because of the economic conditions the Syrians are living and because this reservoir, which is the state, is punctured in many places, so any revenues going into it were syphoned out and so the Syrians were not able to benefit from them.

Dr. Bashar asks: Where did we start fighting corruption? He started with the military establishment. No state starts accountability at the heart of the military establishment during a war; this institution is sacred. However, because it is sacred especially during the war, and because it stands for discipline, this establishment does not allow itself to be, at the same time, be a symbol of corruption. So, accountability started in the military establishment and many high-ranking officers were put in jail with other officers at different levels. Those who were proven innocent were released and there are those who are still being tried up till now and after many years; so, there was no favoritism. The question was raised: is it possible while the military establishment is involved in a war. We said that the military establishment is fighting terrorism and fighting corruption. It fights everything, and because it is the military establishment it should be at the forefront in everything. The same process was also followed in the Ministry of the Interior, the Ministry of Telecommunications. Many institutions were involved. But the issue was raised because there are aspects of society, personalities and institutions which are the subject of people's attentions, in the spotlight of society, the issue was given prominence, while in actual fact, there is nothing new. As to accountability, it is an ongoing process.

According to Al-Assad, as long as there is corruption, fighting it will continue. That is for sure. In these circumstances and in other circumstance. This is part of developing the state. We cannot talk about developing the state in terms of administration and other aspects without fighting corruption. This is self-evident.

Concerning Fighting Corruption

To this issue of corruption, President Assad considers the dereliction or negligence of duty is one thing and corruption is something else. The outcome may be the same sometimes, but here he refers to an official who is not corrupt but is either unable to carry out their duty or does not have a clear vision. When it becomes apparent that they do not have either of these qualities, then they should leave immediately.

At the start of the war the internal situation was not a priority at all to Bashar who used to think of providing the basic needs, just to live, but there was process of tearing up the state and the homeland by terrorists and, on a larger scale, by the corrupt. That was the problem. The country cannot stand it and the state cannot stand it.

Al-Assad continues to say that "We are more interested in actually fighting corruption rather than making a big fuss about it. The legal structure of corruption is the problem, most of the cases referred to the courts are found to be an implementation of the law, which is very vague and has many loopholes. As long as this is the case, even if you are fully-convinced that they are corrupt, they are legally innocent, because they have 'implemented the law.'"

President Bashar says "Our laws give far reaching authorities, and allow for many exemptions. This is why in previous meeting with government, after the reshuffle," the President talked about setting up a committee to amend the laws and in particular cancelling exceptions. Exceptions are not necessarily in the form of allowing for officials to issue them but also in the form that they may implement in various manner at their own discretion. I might implement it in good faith and create discrepancies between people, and I might implement it in bad faith and receive money and consequently become corrupt in the financial sense of the word. That is why we started by focusing on the exceptions given to the President of the Republic. By allowing for exceptions, if I wanted to implement the law fairly, I cannot because I will give you the opportunity to implement the provision in a certain way while somebody else is deprived of this possibility, because I did not encounter him or he did not have access to me. As I said we started by canceling the exceptions of the President of the Republic. Furthermore, any exceptions that are required in particular areas, for example the Customs Law; in these instances, there should be clear boundaries and controls over these exceptions. They should not be left to the discretion of any official regardless of their seniority. So, we used to have so many exceptions without any controls, including in employment and other areas. Again, our laws are full of loopholes which need to be fixed by passing new laws. This has already begun, particularly with local administration laws because the violations we see everywhere are partly legal. This is what we need to do. We are focusing on the anti-corruption law because what we are doing now in terms of fighting corruption is merely addresses the symptoms but does not solve the problem.

To the President, corruption is done in partnership. In the private sector, all those who squandered state money were asked to return it because the objective is to get the money without necessarily being vindictive, before we prosecute and go the courts for years. And we don't know if the courts would be able to return all the money or not. There are documents. Are you prepared to return state money? Many of them expressed a willingness to do so.

The essence in fighting corruption lies in the laws. By disclosing financial assets means this law which will constitute an important reference for any person employed by the state; after one year or twenty years you can ask them how they acquired their assets. People talk about everything except the source of corruption, In Syria, the source lies in the laws and the related executive decrees and measures etc.

Concerning the State of the Syrian Arab Republic

For the President Al-Assad, the Syrian Arab Republic is a state which has basic principles, a constitution, regulations, clear controls. "We are a state, not a sheikhdom as is the case in some countries. The state has a constitution and a law. The first thing in the constitution, or one of its most important provisions, is the protection of private property. We cannot tell somebody, under any title, we take this property. There are many appropriations of properties belonging to terrorists, which have been appropriated temporarily, but they have not become state property, because there is no court decision, although these individuals are terrorists, there is still a need for a court decision. It doesn't mean that this property goes automatically to the state. It needs a court decision. In this framework, the state cannot say, under any title, "you are corrupt, so give me your money." This is at odds with the basic principles of the state."

Concerning the effects of Sanctions

President Bashar Al-Assad says that sanctions have an impact on state revenues in dollars or hard currency in general. This affects the exchange rate, which in turn affects prices. State revenues have also receded as a result of fewer exports and the lack of tourism; no tourists will visit a country during a war. Countries that we depend on for exports are contributing to the sanctions in one way or another. Nonetheless, we have managed to identify unofficial channels for exports, which has contributed to the inflow some hard currency. There is also the speculation game, some of which happens inside Syria and some of which happens outside; additionally, there is speculation on social media, which we get dragged into. The most dangerous of these factors is the psychological.

Bashar wonders why when we hear that the Syrian pound has dropped, we rush to buy dollars. We believe in this way that we have saved money by turning our pounds into dollars, but as a consequence, the exchange rate drops in a severe and accelerated manner and consequently prices rise significantly; what citizens have saved by converting pounds to dollars they have lost due to higher prices. There are many aspects to this issue. Now, can the state intervene? Yes, it can, but with limited revenues and tremendous demand – due to higher prices of basic commodities like wheat, oil, fuel and others, there is a tradeoff between exhausting dollars on speculation or spending on basic needs. If dollars are exhausted, this will mean we will have no wheat and oil; this is our reality. Our revenues are not what they used to be and as such our priorities have been on focused on arms and ammunition and squeezing what we can in order to provide the necessary weapons.

What did the president say in answer to all economic questions is that the solution is there? There are those who say that when I present all these factors, it is because we do not have a solution. No, solutions do exist and are not impossible and what we have done proves that they are not impossible; but this does not mean that we have done our best. This is the starting point and this requires an economic dialogue, I am presenting the larger headlines that we are capable of achieving. Actually, the dollar, the economy and the living conditions are all part of one cycle. They are not separate parts. The solution lies in accelerating state services and facilities to push projects forward and this is what we are doing; we are waiting for a response, because there is a lot of pressure on foreign investors not to invest in Syria.

Currently there is no tourism, so this area will not have an impact on the economic situation, but an agricultural area like the northern regions, this is essential; today we import some of the things which we used to export and because they are imported in a round-about way in order to circumvent the sanctions, we are paying more for them.

For a country like Syria, Al-Assad says "the strength of its economy lies in small and medium-sized enterprises. It is these enterprises, the grocery store or the barber's shop, that will help invigorate the economy. The problem is that some people wait; they say that let us wait to see what happens. If we are to wait, then we should not expect to see the signs that you referred to. Are there signs? Yes, of course, there are improvements, there are industries which have emerged, workshops that have returned to work. The number of people who have returned to the country is higher than the development of the economy, and consequently some might say these improvements are intangible, this is correct. The challenge now is to integrate these people into the economic cycle. The answer to the question: (can we do it?) of course, we can. We should not say that circumstances prevent us, no; we have some laziness, we have some dependencies and sometimes we do not have the vision of how to move. And by we, I mean all of us as a society, as a state and as citizens. The state is responsible to provide the necessary conditions and the infrastructure, but it cannot open all the shops, workshops, and industries."

Furthermore, Syrian President Bashar al-Assad issued a decree on November 21, 2019 to increase the salaries of Syrian government workers and retirees "*The decree provides for an increase of 20,000 Syrian pounds over the monthly salaries and wages of the military and civilians,*" The decree also stipulates an increase of 16,000 Syrian pounds on the salaries of retirees.

The salary increase came after a series of meetings started since the middle of this year between the teams and the competent government committees, and to discuss all the data and data, and after the ratification of the results of the Economic Committee and presented to the Council of Ministers in its last meeting held on November 17, 2019.

Conclusion

During the war years, the Syrian's suffered from high prices, lack of production, shortage of job opportunities, many consequences of terrorism, the sanctions, and the difficult military situation over large parts of the Syrian territory. The natural outcome was a deterioration in the living conditions of Syrian families. But now, conditions on the ground militarily have improved, most of the land has returned to the control of the Syrian state. What about the living conditions? Are there signs of an improvement of this situation, or will the situation remain as it is until all Syrian territory is liberated?

I have high hopes that the role of President Bashar Al-Assad will succeed in fighting corruption, fighting terrorism and building a great and prosperous future for Syria and in moving Syria forward.

Appendix A

Draft Constitution of the Syrian Republic

We, the People of Syria, building on the centuries-long traditions of statehood, proceeding from the responsibility before the past, present and future generations, resolute in our decision to affirm freedom and justice, and confirming our commitment to the Charter of the United Nations Organization, the Charter of the League of Arab States, the Charter of the Organization of Islamic Cooperation, the Universal Declaration of Human Rights, and the Declaration of the Rights of Persons Belonging to National or Ethnic, Religious and Linguistic Minorities, solemnly declare our intention to do the following:

to ensure security, independence, sovereignty and territorial integrity of the state; to live in peace and friendship with other peoples; to successfully establish a civil society; to build a legal democratic state governed by the rule of law as expressed by the will of its people; to ensure a decent standard of living for all in accordance with a just economic and social order.

In the name of the high intention noted above we adopt this Constitution by nation-wide referendum.

Chapter 1. Basic Principles
Article 1

1. The Syrian Republic is an independent sovereign state, based on the principle of the rule of the people by the people and for the people, the rule of law, equality of all before the law, social solidarity, respect for rights and freedoms and equality of rights and duties of all citizens regardless of any differences and privileges. The names Syrian Republic and Syria are equivalent.
2. Syria relies on the unity of its nation and is a common and indivisible homeland for all its citizens. Preserving the national unity and territorial integrity of Syria is the obligation of the State and all its citizens.
3. As a national heritage that promotes national unity, the Constitution shall guarantee the protection of cultural diversity of the Syrian society.

Article 2

1. Syria is a state with a republican form of government.
2. The sole source of power in Syria shall be its multinational and multi faith people. The people shall exercise their sovereign right to freely and independently determine their own destiny. The People of Syria shall exercise their sovereignty in accordance with the Constitution directly by means of a referendum, and through their representatives elected on the basis of universal, equal, direct suffrage by free, secret and personal ballot.
3. Nobody except authorized representatives elected by the people shall have the right to represent the people, speak for the people and make declarations on behalf of the people.
4. No part of the Syrian people, or any social group or organization, or any person may usurp power. The usurpation of power is the gravest crime.

5. No person may simultaneously occupy the position of a member of the People's Assembly, a member of the Constituent Assembly, President of the Republic, Prime Minister, a deputy prime minister, a minister, or a member of the Supreme Constitutional Court.
6. No person carrying another nationality, in addition to the nationality of Syria, may occupy the position of a member of the People's Assembly, a member of the Constituent Assembly, President of the Republic, Prime Minister, a deputy prime minister, a minister, or a member of the Supreme Constitutional Court.
7. The power shall be transferred in a peaceful manner, following a democratic process established by the Constitution and the law.

Article 3

The State shall respect all religions and religious organizations and ensure the freedom to perform all the rituals that do not prejudice public order. Religious organizations shall be equal before the law.

Article 4

1. The official language of the state is Arabic. The law shall regulate how the official language is used.
2. Government agencies and organizations of the Kurdish cultural autonomy shall use Arabic and Kurdish equally.
3. Syrian citizens shall be guaranteed the right to educate their children in their native language in state educational institutions and in private educational institutions that meet the educational standards.
4. Each region shall have the right to use another majority language in addition to the official language as is regulated by the law, if such use was approved by a locally held referendum.

Article 5

1. The political system of the state shall be based on the principle of political pluralism and exercising power democratically by secret ballot.
2. Political parties shall respect the constitutional order, democratic principles, national sovereignty, and territorial integrity of the state.
3. The law shall regulate the provisions and procedures related to the formation of political parties.
4. Public office or public money may not be exploited for a political, electoral or party interest.

Article 6

1. Ideological diversity shall be recognized in Syria. No ideology shall be proclaimed as State ideology or as obligatory. Public associations shall be equal before the law.
2. The State shall ensure security and protect the rights and freedoms of national and religious minorities.
3. The establishment and activities of political parties and other public associations whose goals and activities are aimed at the forcible changing of the basis of the constitutional

order and at violating the integrity of the State, at undermining its security, at engaging in terrorism, at creating armed units, at instigating religious, social, racial, national, and tribal strife; and that are based on sectarian, regional, class, professional discrimination, or on discrimination by gender or origin, may not be undertaken. Such organizations may not be part of the social and political system in Syria.

4. Syria denounces terrorism in all its forms and shall ensure protection of its territories and population against terrorist threats.

Article 7

1. The Constitution shall have supreme legal force, direct effect and shall be applicable in the entire territory of Syria.
2. Laws and other legal acts, which are adopted in Syria, must not contradict the Constitution.
3. Universally recognized principles and norms of international law as well as international agreements of Syria shall be an integral part of its legal system. If an international agreement of Syria establishes rules, which differ from those stipulated by law, then the rules of the international agreement shall be applied.

Article 8

1. Syria shall maintain good neighborly relations with other countries based on cooperation, mutual security and other principles stipulated by international legal rules.
2. Syria denounces war as an infringement on other countries' sovereignty and a means to resolve international conflicts.

Article 9

1. The territory of Syria is indivisible, inviolable and integral.
2. The territory of Syria is inalienable. State borders may be changed only after a referendum among all Syrian citizens, as the expression of the will of the Syrian people.

Article 10

1. It is the State's responsibility, and the duty and obligation of every Syrian citizen to safeguard the homeland's sovereignty, independence, and territorial integrity. In accordance with law, the State shall provide support to the families of citizens who lost their lives while defending independence, sovereignty and territorial integrity of Syria.
2. Citizens of Syria shall perform military service in accordance with law.
3. To defend and safeguard the homeland, the State shall create the army and other armed forces.
4. The army and other armed forces shall be under public oversight and shall defend Syria and its territorial integrity; they may not be used as an instrument of suppression of the people; they may not interfere in politics or participate in the transfer of power.
5. Performing military or militarized activity outside the domain of state power is prohibited.

Article 11

1. In Syria the freedom of economic activity is guaranteed, and private, State, municipal and other forms of property shall be recognized. Property may not be used to infringe on human and civil rights and freedoms, public and State interests, and human dignity.
2. Developing the economy on the basis of different forms of property is aimed at improving the people's wellbeing. The State shall use market principles to bolster economic development, guarantee freedom of entrepreneurship and prevent monopolization and unfair competition in economic relations.
3. The State shall ensure the free flow of goods and financial resources between the regions in accordance with the law.
4. In accordance with the law, land resources may be subject to State, municipal and private ownership.
5. Natural resources shall be publicly owned. The law shall regulate how utilization rights for natural resources or concessions are granted.
6. The law shall regulate taxes and levies. The tax system shall be based on a fair basis.

Article 12

1. The State shall take steps to improve the wellbeing of its people in general and each of its citizens; to guarantee the individual's social security and acceptable living standards.
2. The State shall support development of culture, education, healthcare, science, and art; protect the environment, and safeguard the people's historical, material and spiritual legacy.
3. No discrimination by gender, origin, language or faith shall be allowed.
4. The family shall be the nucleus of society and the State shall protect its existence and its religious, moral and patriotic value. The state shall also protect maternity, childhood and old age, take care of young children and youth and provide the suitable conditions for the development of their talents.
5. The State shall provide women with all opportunities enabling them to effectively and fully contribute to the political, economic, social and cultural life, and the State shall work on removing the restrictions that prevent their development and participation in building society.
6. Children shall have the right to be brought up, taken care of and educated by their parents. Parents shall be entitled to respect and care from their children, especially when parents require it, or due to an inability to work or because of old age.
7. Slavery, trafficking in women and children, exploitation of children is prohibited and shall be prosecuted by law.
8. Following a court's decision individuals may be sentenced to compulsory labor the terms and duration of which are regulated by law. Compulsory labor may also be ordered by authorities during military service, and during the state of emergency – for the kinds of labor as stipulated by law.

Article 13

1. Public service shall be a responsibility and an honor the purpose of which is to achieve public interest and to serve the people.

2. Citizens shall be equal in assuming the functions of public service. The law shall determine the conditions of assuming such functions and the rights and duties assigned to them.

Article 14

1. Protection of the environment shall be the responsibility of the state and society and it shall be the duty of every citizen.
2. The State and the public shall share responsibility when managing natural and manmade disasters.

Article 15

1. Syria consists of constituent parts.
2. The law states the number of constituent parts, their boundaries and status.
3. The organization of local administrations is based on applying the principle of decentralization of authorities and responsibilities. The law states the relationship between these units and the central authority, their mandate, financial revenues and control over their work. It also states the way such administrations are appointed or elected.
4. The law shall state the status of the Kurdish Cultural Autonomy.

Article 16

1. The monetary unit in Syria shall be the Syrian pound (lira).
2. The National Bank of Syria is owned exclusively by the State and shall have the right to emit money and withdraw it from circulation.

Article 17

1. The capital of the state is Damascus.
2. The flag of Syria consists of three colors: red, white and black, in addition to two stars, each with five heads of green color. The flag is rectangular in shape; its width equals two thirds of its length and consists of three rectangles evenly spaced along the flag, the highest in red, the middle in white and the lowest in black, and the two stars are in the middle of the white rectangle.
3. The law identifies the state's emblem and its national anthem.
4. In cases provided for by the Constitution and/or by law citizens shall give the following oath: "I swear to observe the country's Constitution, to respect and protect human and civil rights and freedoms, to safeguard the State's sovereignty, independence, and territorial integrity, and to always act in the interests of the Syrian people."

Chapter 2. Human and Civil Rights and Freedoms
Article 18

1. Everyone shall have the right to life, security and freedom and the State shall guarantee these rights. No right can be restricted or denied to a person unless otherwise provided by law and following the decision by the appropriate judicial authority.

2. All persons shall be equal before the law without discrimination among them on grounds of gender, race, nationality, origin, color, religion, personal convictions, beliefs or views, and economic and social status.

Article 19

1. Everyone shall have the right to participate in the political, economic, social and cultural life.
2. Citizens, men and women, shall have the right to participate in managing State affairs and exercise their political rights including the right to elect and be elected.
3. No person shall be coerced to become a member of any party, association, society or political organization, or to keep his or her membership in said organizations.
4. Everyone shall respect and observe the Constitutions and laws.

Article 20

1. Everyone shall be guaranteed freedom of thought and speech, and freedom of conscience and religion. Nobody shall be forced to express his thoughts and convictions or to deny them.
2. The State shall guarantee the freedom of conscience and the protection of places of worship. Sacred shrines and religious sanctuaries shall be considered places of religious and cultural importance, and the State shall assume the responsibility to safeguard and protect them.
3. Everyone shall have the right to participate for lawful purposes in meetings, peaceful rallies and strikes.
4. Everyone shall have the right freely to seek, receive, transmit, produce and disseminate information by any legal means. In accordance with the law the State ensures freedom of the press and mass media.
5. Propaganda or agitation, which incites social, racial, national or religious hatred and hostility, and propaganda of social, racial, national, religious or linguistic supremacy, shall be prohibited.

Article 21

1. The law shall regulate the Syrian citizenship.
2. A citizen of Syria may not be deprived of his (her) citizenship.
3. A citizen of Syria may not be deported from Syria or extradited to another state.
4. Every citizen may freely enter and leave Syria unless otherwise stipulated by law and expressed in an applicable decision of the court or the prosecutor's office.
5. Persons who are persecuted for their political convictions may not be extradited to other states.
6. Syria shall guarantee protection and patronage to its citizens living abroad permanently or temporarily.

Article 22

1. Everyone shall have the right to the inviolability of his (her) person, home, personal and family privacy.

2. Collecting, keeping, using and disseminating information about the private life of a person shall not be permitted without his (her) consent.
3. The State shall guarantee a person's right to privacy of correspondence, of telephone conversations and of postal, telegraph and other communications. This right may be limited by law to prevent a crime or to uncover the truth when investigating a crime.
4. Except when the law says otherwise or when following a court's order, nobody may enter a home against the will of its occupants.

Article 23

1. Everyone shall have the right to property.
2. Property rights, including individual private ownership, shall be protected by law.
3. Nobody may be deprived of property except under a court order. Private ownership may be removed in the State or public interest only against fair compensation according to the law.
4. The State shall guarantee the right of inheritance in accordance with the law.

Article 24

1. Labor is the basis for personal and public prosperity. Everyone shall have the right to freely choose the type of activity, occupation and place of work based on his (her) skills. The State shall use all means at its disposal to eliminate unemployment.
2. Everyone shall have the right to work in conditions, which meet safety and hygiene requirements, and to receive remuneration for labor without any discrimination whatsoever.
3. Everyone shall have the right to rest. For those working under labor contracts the duration of work time, days of rest and public holidays and annual paid leave established by federal law shall be guaranteed.
4. The law shall regulate employer-employee relations based on economic principles and the norms of social justice.
5. The State shall guarantee the right of its people to lawfully form labor associations and unions and to join them.
6. Individual and collective labor disputes are to be resolved in a manner stated by law.

Article 25

Everyone shall be obliged to pay legally established taxes and levies.

Article 26

1. Everyone shall be guaranteed social security payments for legal retirement age, in case of illness, disability, loss of breadwinner, incapacitation, unemployment, and in other cases specified by law. Minimum state pensions and social benefits shall be established by law.
2. Helping people in need is the obligation of his (her) family members.
3. The State shall facilitate development of charity movements, voluntary social insurance programs and other forms of social security.

Article 27

1. Everyone shall have the right to participate in cultural life and use cultural establishments and access cultural valuables.
2. Everyone shall respect the historical, cultural and spiritual heritage; take care of it and protect historical and cultural monuments.

Article 28

1. Everyone has the right to health protection and medical care in state and municipal health institutions.
2. The State shall take the necessary measures to develop all forms of health services based on various forms of property and guarantee sanitary and epidemiological well-being.

Article 29

1. Everyone shall have the right to education. The State shall guarantee free secondary education. The law shall specify cases when a person can receive free secondary vocational and higher education.
2. The education system is controlled by the State.
3. The State shall encourage and promote physical culture and sport. It shall also provide everything needed for such purposes.
4. The state shall support scientific research and guarantee the freedom of scientific, literary, artistic, and cultural creative activity. It shall also provide for the development of talents and abilities and allocate the funds necessary for such purposes.
5. The State shall encourage scientific and technological inventions, creative skills and talents and protect their results.

Article 30

1. No one can be unlawfully deprived of a home.
2. The State shall promote housing construction and create conditions for exercising the right to a home.

Article 31

1. Punishment shall be personal; no crime and no punishment except by a law.
2. Anyone shall be considered innocent until his (her) guilt is proven and confirmed by a court sentence which has entered into legal force.
3. The right to conduct litigation and remedies, review, and the defense before the judiciary shall be protected by the law, and the state shall guarantee legal aid to those who are incapable to do so, in accordance with the law
4. No immunity of any act or administrative decision from judicial review shall be allowed.
5. A law, which introduces or increases liability, shall not have retroactive force.

Article 32

1. No one may be investigated or arrested, except under an order or decision issued by the competent judicial authority, or if he was arrested in the case of being caught in the act, or with the intent to bring him to the judicial authorities on charges of committing a felony or misdemeanor.
2. No one may be tortured or treated in a humiliating manner, and the law shall define the punishment for those who do so.
3. Any person who is arrested must be informed of the reasons for his arrest and his rights and may not be incarcerated except by an order of the competent judicial authority.
4. Any person sentenced by a final ruling, who has carried out his sentence and the ruling proved wrong shall have the right to ask the state for compensation for the damage he suffered.

Article 33

Any assault on individual freedom, on the inviolability of private life or any other rights and public freedoms guaranteed by the Constitution shall be considered a crime punishable by law.

Chapter 3. Legislative Authority
Article 34

The legislative authority is assumed on behalf of the Syrian people by the People's Assembly and the Constituent Assembly in the manner prescribed by the Constitution and applicable laws.

Article 35

1. Members of the People's Assembly shall be elected by the public, secret, direct and equal vote. They shall represent the whole people of Syria.
2. The People's Assembly term shall be four calendar years from the date of its first meeting
3. The People's Assembly shall continue to meet and exercise legislative authority until the new People's Assembly is elected and holds its first meeting.
4. If the membership of a member of the People's Assembly is vacant for some reason, an alternative shall be elected within sixty days from the date of the membership vacancy, provided that the remaining term of the People's Assembly is no less than six months. The membership of the new member shall end by the expiry date of the mandate of the Assembly's term. The Election Law shall determine the cases of vacant membership.

Article 36

1. The system of electing members of the People's Assembly, their number and status shall be determined by a law.
2. Voters shall be the citizens who have completed eighteen years of age and meet the conditions stipulated in the Election Law.
3. The Election Law shall include the provisions that ensure:

1. the freedom and safety of voters, the right to choose their representatives and the integrity of the electoral procedures;
2. the right of candidates to supervise the electoral process;
3. liability for those who abuse the will of the voters;
4. identifying the regulations of financing election campaigns;
5. organization of the election campaign and the use of media outlets.
6. Elections shall be held during the sixty days preceding the expiry date of the mandate of the People's Assembly term.

Article 37

1. The Supreme Constitutional Court shall have jurisdiction to consider appeals related to the elections of the members of the People's Assembly.
2. Appeals shall be submitted by the candidate within three days from the date of announcing the results; and the court shall make its final judgment within seven days from the expiry date of submitting appeals.

Article 38

1. The People's Assembly shall convene following a decree of the President of the Republic within fifteen days after the mandate of the current People's Assembly expires.
2. The People's Assembly shall meet on the sixteenth day after the mandate of the current People's Assembly expires, if there is no decree by the President of the Republic.

Article 39

1. The People's Assembly shall call for three regular sessions per year; the total of which should not be less than six months, and the Assembly's rules of procedure shall set the time and duration of each of them.
2. The People's Assembly may be invited to extraordinary sessions upon the request of the Speaker, of one third or more of the members of the People's Assembly, or of the President of the Republic.
3. The last legislative session of the year shall remain open until the approval of the state budget.

Article 40

1. The Constituent Assembly shall be formed to ensure participation of representatives of the constituent parts in legislative activities and administration of the state.
2. The Constituent Assembly consists of representatives of the constituent parts.
3. The law shall specify how members of the Constituent Assembly are delegated, their number, status and term of service.

Article 41

1. The People's Assembly and the Constituent Assembly hold sessions separately.

2. The People's Assembly and the Constituent Assembly may meet together to elect and to hear the Prime Minister, the President of the Republic, speeches of leaders of foreign states, and in other cases specified by the Constitution and law.
3. The People's Assembly and the Constituent Assembly shall adopt the rules of procedure to coordinate their work and exercise authority.
4. The People's Assembly and the Constituent Assembly elect speakers from among their members. In accordance with the rules of procedure the speakers shall represent the Assemblies and perform organizational functions.
5. The People's Assembly and the Constituent Assembly may form committees from among their members to deal with the issues related to exercising their authority.

Article 42

1. In carrying out their duties, the members of the People's Assembly and the Constituent Assembly shall be guided by the Constitution, and their mandate can be restricted only in accordance with the Constitution.
2. The members of the People's Assembly and the Constituent Assembly shall not use their mandate for personal gain outside the focus of their activity. A law shall specify activities that cannot be combined with the mandate of a member of People's Assembly and a member of the Constituent Assembly.
3. The members of the People's Assembly and the Constituent Assembly cannot be held legally responsible for their votes or political opinions expressed in exercising their authority.
4. Before taking office the members of the People's Assembly and the Constituent Assembly shall give the constitutional oath stated in Article 17 of the Constitution.
5. A member of People's Assembly and a member of the Constituent Assembly cannot be detained, arrested, searched or brought before the court without a prior permission from the Assembly to which he belongs.
6. A member of People's Assembly and a member of the Constituent Assembly caught in the act may be detained and searched. The Minister of Justice shall immediately notify the Speaker of the respective Assembly about the detention and search. If the notified Assembly (and, if the Assembly is not in session, the Speaker) states that there are no grounds for detention, the measure shall be canceled immediately. If the Assembly is not in session, the Speaker of the Assembly shall call it for a special session to consider initiating criminal proceedings against the member of the Assembly and applying restraining measures.
7. The emoluments and compensations to members of the People's Assembly and the Constituent Assembly shall be determined by a law.

Article 43

The People's Assembly undertakes the following functions:

1) approval of laws;
2) calling an election of the President of the Republic;
3) performing a vote of no-confidence to the government;
4) ratification of international agreements and conventions;

5) approval of international treaties and agreements, granting privileges to foreign companies, approval of international treaties and agreements entailing additional expenses not included in the budget, or contracts and agreements related to state loans, or those that require new legislation to become effective;
6) approval of a general amnesty;
7) deciding whether to terminate the mandate of an Assembly member.

Article 44

1. The Constituent Assembly performs the following functions:
   1) approval of laws;
   2) performing a vote of no-confidence to the government;
   3) resolving issues of war and peace;
   4) terminating the mandate of the President of the Republic;
   5) approval of the President's decision to declare the state of emergency or mobilization;
   6) appointment of judges of the Supreme Constitutional Court;
   7) appointment and dismissal of the Chairman of the National Bank of Syria;
   8) deciding whether to terminate the mandate of an Assembly member.

Article 45

1. The legislative initiative belongs to the members of the People's Assembly, of the Constituent Assembly, the President of the Republic and the Government.
2. Upon the request by administration of a territorial unit the Constituent Assembly shall have the right to send bills to the People's Assembly for consideration.
3. Bills shall be submitted to the People's Assembly.

Article 46

1. Laws shall be adopted by the People's Assembly.
2. A law is adopted by a majority vote of all deputies of the People's Assembly.
3. Laws adopted by the People's Assembly shall be submitted within five days to the Territories Assembly for consideration.
4. A law is considered approved by the Constituent Assembly, if more than half of the total number of its members voted in favor of it.
5. If the Constituent Assembly rejects the law a conciliatory commission may be set up by the Assemblies to resolve differences, whereupon the law shall be reconsidered by the Constituent Assembly.
6. If the People's Assembly disagrees with the decision of the Constituent Assembly, the law shall pass if at least two thirds of the total number of deputies of the People's Assembly voted for it the second ballot.
7. The law approved or adopted in the second ballot shall within five days be forwarded to the President of the Republic, who shall sign it and promulgate it within fourteen days.
8. The President of the Republic has the right to reject the law within fourteen days after receiving it. In this case the People's Assembly and the Constituent Assembly shall have the right to reconsider the law. If after the reconsideration the law is approved in its earlier

adopted edition by at least two thirds of the total number of members of the People's Assembly and the Constituent Assembly, it shall be signed and promulgated by the President of the Republic within seven days.

Article 47

1. For every fiscal year there shall be one budget; and the beginning of a fiscal year shall be determined by a law. Appropriations cannot be transferred from one title to another except according to the provisions of the law.
2. The Government shall submit the draft budget to the People's Assembly at least two months before the beginning of the fiscal year.
3. The budget shall be considered, approved, signed and promulgated in the order prescribed by Article 46 of the Constitution. The People's Assembly shall vote separately on each title of the budget.
4. If the process of approving and promulgating the budget is not complete before the beginning of the new fiscal year, the budget of the previous years is used until the new year budget is approved, and the revenues are collected in accordance with the laws and regulations in force.
5. The budget may be approved together with laws which could create new expenditures and new revenues to cover them.
6. The final accounts of the fiscal year shall be presented by the Government to the People's Assembly within a period not longer than one year as of the end of this year.

Chapter 4. The Executive Authority
Article 48

The President of the Republic and the Government of the Republic exercise executive authority on behalf of the people within the limits provided for in the Constitution.

Article 49

1. The President of the Republic is elected for the term of 7 years by citizens of Syria on the basis of universal, equal, and direct suffrage by secret ballot.
2. No person can hold the office of the President of the republic for more than two consecutive terms.
3. The candidate who wins the election for the President of the Republic is the one who gets more than one half of votes of those who take part in the elections. If no candidate receives such majority, a rerun is carried out between the two candidates who receive the largest number of votes.
4. The results shall be announced by the Speaker of the People's Assembly.
5. If the President's term in office has expired and no new President has been elected, the existing President of the Republic continues to assume his duties until the new President is elected.

Article 50

A candidate for the presidency must be over 40 years of age and hold the Syrian citizenship.

Article 51

1. The nomination of a candidate for the office of President of the Republic shall be as follows:
   1) The People's Assembly calls for the election of the President of the Republic within a period not less than 30 days and not more than 90 days before the end of the term of office of the existing president;
   2) the candidacy application shall be made to the Supreme Constitutional Court and entered in a special register within 10 days of announcing the call for electing the president;
   3) the candidacy application shall not be accepted unless the applicant has acquired the support of at least 35 members of the People's Assembly and (or) the Constituent Assembly. No member of the Assemblies can support more than one candidate;
   4) applications shall be examined by the Supreme Constitutional Court; and should be ruled on within 5 days of the deadline for application.
2. If the conditions required for candidacy were met by only one candidate during the period set for applying, the Speaker of the People's Assembly decides on the postponement of the elections of the President of the Republic and calls for fresh nominations according to the same conditions.

Article 52

1. The Supreme Constitutional Court has the jurisdiction to examine the challenges to the election of the President of the Republic.
2. The challenges shall be made by the candidate within 3 days of announcing the results; and the court makes a final ruling on them within 7 days after the deadline for making the challenges.

Article 53

Before assuming his duties, the President of the Republic shall be sworn in before the People's Assembly and the Constituent Assembly by saying the constitutional oath mentioned in Article 17 of the Constitution.

Article 54

The allocations required for the office of the President of the Republic shall be set out in the budget.

Article 55

1. The President of the Republic is the guarantor of the independence, unity and territorial integrity of the country.

2. The President of the Republic shall enforce the Constitution, ensure continuous operation of public authorities, and protect the constitutional order, national sovereignty and territorial integrity.
3. The President of the Republic shall act as an intermediary for the state authorities, and between the state and the society. To resolve disputes between the state bodies, the President has the right to use conciliatory procedures.
4. The President of the Republic represents Syria in international relations.
5. The President of the Republic shall decide on issues of citizenship and granting of political asylum, award state medals and honors, confer supreme military ranks and supreme special titles; and grant pardon.

Article 56

The President of the Republic has the right to address letters to the People's Assembly and the Constituent Assembly, as well as make statements before them.

Article 57

The President of the Republic issues decrees, edicts and instructions in accordance with the Constitution and the law.

Article 58

1. The President of the Republic shall conclude international treaties on behalf of Syria and refer them to the People's Assembly for ratification.
2. Upon proposal from the government, the President shall appoint and recall diplomatic representatives of Syria and approves the establishment and abolition of or change of status for diplomatic missions.
3. The President accepts credentials and letters of recall of accredited heads of foreign diplomatic missions.

Article 59

The President of the Republic might call for a referendum on important issues which affect the higher interests of the country. The result of the referendum shall be binding and come into force as of the date of its announcement by the President of the Republic.

Article 60

1. The President of the Republic is the Commander in Chief of the army and armed forces; and he issues all the decisions necessary to exercise this authority.
2. In the event of aggression or threat of aggression against Syria, the President of the Republic shall:
   1) take measures to repel the aggression and immediately notify the People's Assembly and the Constituent Assembly of such measures in an address. In case the People's Assemble

and the Constituent Assembly are not in session, they are to be summoned within 24 hours after the beginning of the aggression;

2) declare mobilization and within 3 days of such declaration ask the Constituent Assembly to approve it.

3. In the event of aggression or threat of aggression against Syria, or threats to the security of the state, the President shall have the right to declare the state of emergency in the territory of the country or in its certain parts with prior approval from the Constituent Assembly. In exceptional cases the decision of the President of the Republic is sent for approval to the Constituent Assembly within a day after making such a decision. When the state of emergency is in effect, the People's Assembly, the Constituent Assembly and the President of the Republic shall continue to exercise their authority. Besides, the no-confidence vote cannot be made to the government.

Article 61

1. The President of the Republic may be removed from office by the Constituent Assembly only after the People's Assembly brings against him charges of high treason or another grave crime, and the legality of such charges and of the procedure for bringing them up have been confirmed in the Supreme Constitutional Court's resolution.

2. The decision of the People's Assembly to bring up charges and the decision of the Constituent Assembly to remove the President from office must be made by two thirds of all the votes of the members of each Assembly following the initiative from at least one third of the members of the People's Assembly.

3.   The decision of the Constituent Assembly to remove the President of the Republic must be adopted not later than ninety days after the People's Assembly brings up the charges against the President. If within this period the Constituent Assembly fails to adopt such a decision, the charges against the President shall be regarded as rejected.

Article 62

1. If the office of the President of the Republic becomes vacant or if he is permanently incapacitated, the Prime Minister assumes the President's duties for a period of no more than 90 days of the President of the Republic's office becoming vacant or his permanent incapacitation. When the Prime Minister is unable to perform such duties, the functions of the President are delegated to the Speaker of the Constituent Assembly. Within the stated period of time new presidential elections shall be held.

2. In case of resignation, the President of the Republic shall inform the People's Assembly and the Constituent Assembly about it.

Article 63

1. The Government is the highest executive body. It consists of the Prime Minister, his deputies and ministers. The government shall control the implementation of laws and development plans, and the work of state bodies.

2. The Government shall be responsible before the President of the Republic, the People's Assembly and the Constituent Assembly.

3. The President of the Republic determines the general directions of the Government activities. He has the right to summon the Government for a meeting, to preside at the government meetings, to request reports from the Prime Minister, his deputies and ministers.
4. The Prime Minister manages the Government, coordinates and controls the work of his deputies and ministers, speaks on behalf of the Government.

Article 64

1. The President of the Republic appoints the Prime Minister, his deputies and ministers, accepts their resignations and dismisses them.
2. The President shall appoint deputies to the Prime Minister and ministers based on the proportionate representation of all ethnic and religious groups of the Syrian population; some positions shall be reserved for national and religious minorities. Regarding these issues the President of the Republic has the right to hold consultations with the members of the People's Assembly and the Constituent Assembly.

Article 65

The Prime Minister, his deputies and ministers are sworn in before the President of the Republic by saying the constitutional oath stated in Article 17 of the Constitution.

Article 67

1. Within thirty days after the formation of the Government, the Prime Minister shall submit the program of actions to the People's Assembly and to the Constituent Assembly for discussion at a joint session.
2. Members of the People's Assembly and the Constituent Assembly have the right to send inquiries to the Government, the Prime Minister, his deputies and ministers according to the assembly's rules of procedure.

Article 67

The mandate of the Government is as follows:
1) it guides the work of ministries and other public bodies;
2) it drafts the state budget;
3) it drafts laws;
4) it draws executive plans of the Government;
5) it concludes loans agreements, provides state guarantees and credits in accordance with the budget;
6) it concludes international treaties and agreements granting privileges to foreign companies, international treaties and agreements entailing additional expenses not included in the budget, or contracts and agreements related to loans, or those that require new legislation to become effective;
7) it oversees implementation of the laws, protecting the interests and security of the state, the rights and freedoms of the population;

8) it makes administrative decisions in accordance with the law and overseeing their implementation;

9) it appoints and dismisses civil servants and servicemen in accordance with the law.

Article 68

1. The Government issues decisions and regulations.
2. Decisions are issued in the furtherance of the laws.
3. Regulations shall be based on a law giving the Government authority to issue such a regulation.

Article 69

1. The Prime Minister, his deputies and ministers are forbidden from being on the boards of private companies or from representing such companies, as well as from engaging in direct and indirect commercial activities and private entrepreneurship.
2. The law shall state what responsibilities shall be imposed on the Prime Minister, his deputies and ministers to prevent and resolve a conflict of interest.

Article 70

The People's Assembly, the Constituent Assembly and the President of the Republic have the right to call for criminal prosecution of the Prime Minister, his deputies and ministers for acts committed by them while exercising authority. Bringing a member of the government before the court leads to his suspension from his office.

Article 71

1. The government shall resign in the following cases:
   1) upon expiration of the term of office of the President of the Republic;
   2) in case of a vote of no confidence;
2. The government shall continue its work until a new government is formed.

Article 72

1. The People's Assembly and the Constituent Assembly may obtain a no confidence vote in the Government at a joint session by a majority of votes of all the members of the People's Assembly and the Constituent Assembly.
2. The no confidence vote may be initiated by no less than one third of all the members of the People's Assembly or by no less than one third of all the members of the Constituent Assembly. The government shall be informed of the vote on the day of such proposal.
3. The no confidence vote is submitted for discussion three days after the initial proposal at a joint session of the People's Assembly and the Constituent Assembly.
4. If the no confidence vote is rejected, the members of the People's Assembly or the members of the Constituent Assembly who initiated the vote cannot initiate a new no confidence vote during the term of the People's Assembly.

Chapter 5. The Judicial Authority
Article 73

1. Judges are independent and there is no authority over them except that of the constitution and law.
2. The judges' honor, conscience and impartiality constitute the guarantees for people's rights and freedoms.
3. Judicial rulings are made in the name of the people of Syria.

Article 74

1. The judicial system and courts' powers are defined by law.
2. The law states the conditions for appointing judges, promoting, transferring, disciplining and dismissing them.

Article 75

The Attorney General's Office is the single judicial institution headed by the Minister of Justice. The law regulates its function and mandate.

Article 76

The State's Council is in charge of Administrative Judiciary. It is an independent judicial and advisory body. The law states its mandate and the status of The State's Council members.

Article 77

1. The Supreme Constitutional Court is an independent judicial body based in Damascus.
2. The Supreme Constitutional Court consists of at least seven judges, appointed by the Constituent Assembly.
3. In addition to the public offices stated by the Constitution, the law may indicate other positions and offices that are incompatible with the position of a judge on the Supreme Constitutional Court.
4. The term in office of a Supreme Constitutional Court judge shall be four years and renewable.
5. Judges of the Supreme Constitutional Court cannot be dismissed except when the law allows it.
6. President and members of the Supreme Constitutional Court before they assume office shall be sworn in before the People's Assembly and the Constituent Assembly by saying "I swear to respect the Constitution and the laws of the country and to carry out my duties with integrity and impartiality."

Article 78

1. The mandate of the Supreme Constitutional Court is as follows:
   1) Control over the constitutionality of laws, decrees, bylaws and regulations of public authorities.

2) Expressing opinion, upon the request of the President of the Republic, on the constitutionality of draft laws and the legality of draft decrees.
3) Overseeing the election of the President of the Republic and organizing the relevant procedure.
4) Considering challenges against the election of the President of the Republic and ruling on these challenges.
5) Trying the President of the Republic who was removed from the office after committing high treason or another grave crime.

2. The law shall specify other authority of the Supreme Constitutional Court and the process for considering and ruling on the issues under the mandate of the Supreme Constitutional Court, and the status of judges on the Supreme Constitutional Court.

Article 79

The Supreme Constitutional Court shall not consider the constitutionality of laws put to a referendum that have received the approval of the people.

Chapter 6. Amending the Constitution
Article 80

1. A proposal for amending the Constitution can be submitted to the People's Assembly by at least a third of the members of the People's Assembly, or by at least a third of the members of the Constituent Assembly, or by the President of the Republic.
2. To be considered final, the proposal for amending the Constitution must be approved by a three quarters majority of the People's Assembly, endorsed by a three quarters majority of the Constituent Assembly, then signed by the President of the Republic and promulgated.
3. If the proposal for amending the Constitution is not endorsed by the Constituent Assembly, such proposal shall be withdrawn and not considered further.

Chapter 7. Concluding and Transitional Provisions
Article 81

Laws and other legal acts passed before this Constitution comes into force shall apply until amended in accordance with the Constitution. The respective amendments shall be made within no longer than one year from the date the Constitution comes into force.

Article 82

The term in office of the current President of the Republic shall be 7 years from the swearing-in date. He has the right to run again for President of the Republic. The President's term in office as stated in this Constitution shall apply to him as of the next presidential elections.

Article 83

Elections for the first People's Assembly under this Constitution shall be held after the term of the previous People's Assembly expires.

Article 84

The Constituent Assembly shall be formed within no more than one year from the date the Constitution comes into force.

Article 85

The Constitution shall come into force on the day of its promulgation after the referendum.

REFERENCES

Agence France-Presse (AFP), January 29,2019

Al-Assad Parliament speech on July 7, 2017

BBC, *"UN envoy calls for transitional government in Syria"*, June 30th 2012

BBC, *"Syria conflict: sides trade blame over talks' suspension"*, February 4th 2016.

Bergen, Peter L., "The Osama bin Laden I know" Free Press, a division of Simon & Schuster, Inc. New York, 2006

Clark, Wesley "In Winning Modern Wars: Iraq, Terrorism and The American Empire", PublicAffairs; 1st US - 1st Printing edition (October 16, 2003)

Chossudovsky, Michel, "SYRIA: Who is Behind the Protest Movement?" Fabricating a Pretext for a US-NATO Humanitarian Intervention, Global Research, May 3, 2011.

Collier, Paul and Sambanis, Nicholas *"Understand Civil War"*, Volume 1: Africa, the World Bank Publication, 2005

Concard, Lawrence, *"The Conquest of Arwad: A Source-Critical Study in the Historiography of the Early Medieval Near East,"* Book Chapter, 1992

Ettarah, Jamil, *"Think Palestine: To Unlock U.S. Israelis & Arabs Conflicts"* (vol. one) AuthorHouse, Bloomington, Indiana, 2007

Cunningham, Finian, **"False-Flag Failure... US Cuts to the Chase to Defend Its Terrorists in Syria",** RT News, September 7, 2018

Dalacoura, Katerina. *"Islamic Terrorism and Democracy in the Middle East"*, Cambridge University Press. 2011

Foreign affairs and international relations, *European Council: "Supporting the future of Syria and the region: co-chairs declaration"* May, 2017

Gerges, Fawaz A., *"ISIS: A History"*, Princeton University Press, April 2016

Indian Punchline, November 20,.2018

Kraeling C. H. (With contributions by Torrey C. C., Welles C. B., and Geiger B.), *"Final Report VIII. Part I. The Synagogue,"* Yale University Press, New Haven, and Oxford University Press, London, 1956

Kurdish media network (Rudaw), *"Geneva V ends with UN mediator pleading for ceasefire in Syria"*, March 31, 2017

Landau, Noa, *"Netanyahu: Israel Has No Problem with Assad, but Cease-fire Agreements Must Be Upheld,"* Haaretz, July 12, 2018.

Liz Zulliani, "Economic Watch: follow the money", March 20, 2011 www.economywatch.com/world_economy/syria/structure-of-economy.html)

Rabinowitz, Gavin *"Liberman says Assad is a 'butcher' who must go,"* Times of Israel, December15, 2016.

RadioFreeEurope, *"Russia Plans to Help Syria Rebuild Devastated Oil, Power Industries"* February 14, 2018

Reuters, "Russia and Syria say opposition trying to wreck peace talks", March 2nd 2017

Reuter's reporting on June 4, 2018 from Beirut, Lebanon

Russian News Agency (TASS), October 30, 2018.

Russian News Agency (TASS), November 13, 2018.

Russian News Agency (TASS), November 30, 2018

Russian News Agency (TASS), December 6, 2018.

Russian News Agency (TASS), December 8, 2018.

Syrian Arab News Agency *(SANA) "Damascus International Fair to be held against all odds"* 24 May 2017

Syrian Arab News (SANA) December 4, and 5, 2018.

Syrian Arab News (SANA) October 31, 2019.

Syrian Arab News Agency, *"the Arab Forum on Confronting Zionist-US Reactionary forces Alliance to be Held in Damascus"*, Damascus, November 12, 2017

syriasolidritymovement.org of the Syria Solidarity Movement on May 27, 2018.

Tillerson, Rex W.'s speech, Hoover Institute at Stanford University, Stanford, CA, January 17, 2018

The daily Star, *"Jihadists force Syria Christian to convert at gunpoint"*, September 11, 2013

Valiente, Alexander, *"President Assad's Speech at the Arab Forum for Confronting the Zionist-US Reactionary Alliance,"* Internationalist News, Syria November 14, 2017

Voice of Russia, June 17, 2011

Wang Jin, *"Will China Pay for Syria to Rebuild?"* The Diplomat, February 16, 2017

Wintour, Patrick, *"Putin brings Iran and Turkey together in bold Syria peace plan,"* the Guardian, November 22, 2017

Yassin-Kassab, Robin and Leila Al-Shami *"Burning Country: Syrians in Revolution and War"* – Paperback – February 15, 2016, ISBN-10:0745337821

Printed in the United States
By Bookmasters